POWER LEARNING

A STUDENT'S GUIDE TO SUCCESS

For Ro Griffiths, Noel Scott
and the Teacher-Librarians
who worked to restore
Teacher-Librarianship
for New Zealand

POWER LEARNING

A STUDENT'S GUIDE TO SUCCESS

GWEN GAWITH

MILLS
PUBLICATIONS

First publication 1991
Reprinted 1991
MILLS PUBLICATIONS
P O Box 30-818 Lower Hutt
New Zealand

ISBN 0-908722-90-7

Edited by Anna Rogers
Illustrated by Gwen Gawith
Designed and Typeset by The Creative Company, Wellington
Cover design by Phillip Andrews, Freelance Group, Wellington
Printed in Hong Kong through Bookprint Consultants, Wellington

Contents

Author

Gwen Gawith M.A. (Library & Information Studies), Cert. Art, Dip. Lib., Dip. Ed., is an Auckland based lecturer, author and illustrator. She draws on a background of graphic art, management, marketing, librarianship and teaching to develop courses and resources which make research, reading and learning enjoyable for all ages.

Gwen Gawith has an international reputation as an educator. Her books *Library Alive, Information Alive, Action Learning, Reading Alive* are recommended texts in the U.K., Australia and New Zealand.

Introduction

Power Learning is based on a single and simple belief:

➧ that anyone and everyone can learn to learn more by learning to control the learning process.

- *Power Learning* gives you the power to control your own learning.
- *Power Learning* shows you how you can harness learning skills (planning, reading, research, notemaking, writing, presentation) into the easy 12-part *Power Learning* process.
- *Power Learning* shows you the key strategies which drive this process.
- *Power Learning* shows you how to manage your time so that these learning skills and strategies become a habit.
- *Power Learning* teaches you easy to remember recipes for applying these learning skills and strategies.
- *Power Learning* shows you how to direct these skills and strategies to meet the particular needs of a particular stage of the learning process.

Power Learning works on the assumption that learning is not just a matter of mastering different skills such as notemaking, essay writing, reading, thinking, etc. Learning is a process. All these skills combine, like the parts of a car engine, into a process. You, as the learner, need to learn to drive this process.

This diagram shows the plan of the book.

- Power Learning is broken into 12 sections. Each section focuses on a key skill area.
- Each skill section is self contained. So if you want to target particular skills or techniques, turn straight to the relevant section.

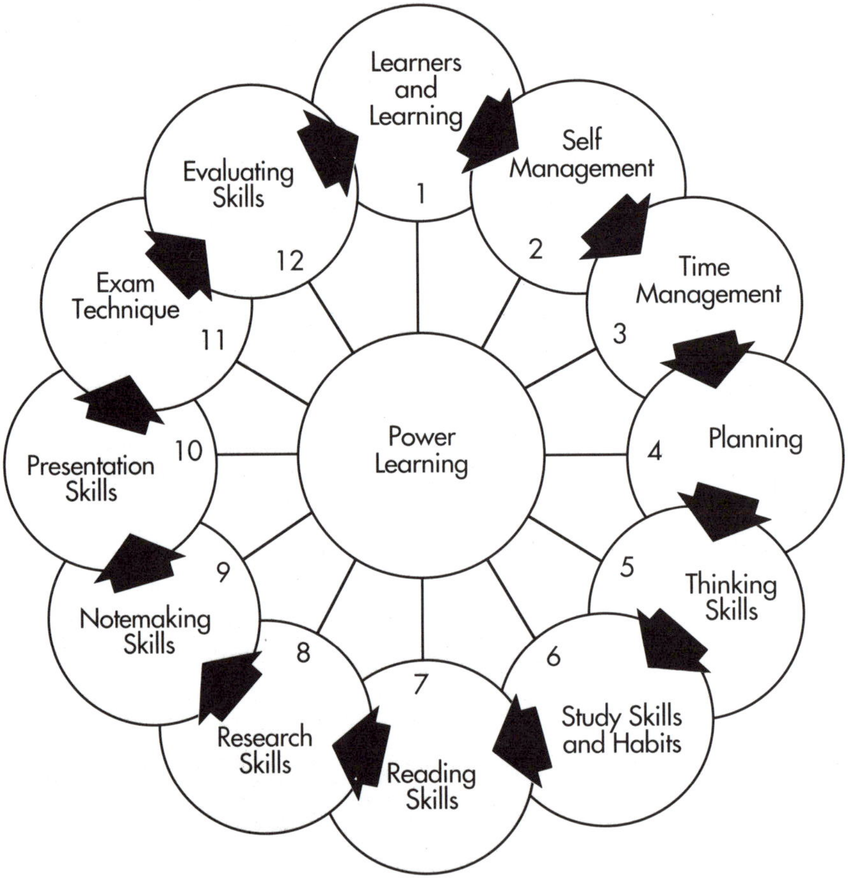

Each section is structured around focus questions. By asking these, you start to control your learning. Taken together, these sections and questions represent a map of the *Power Learning* process.

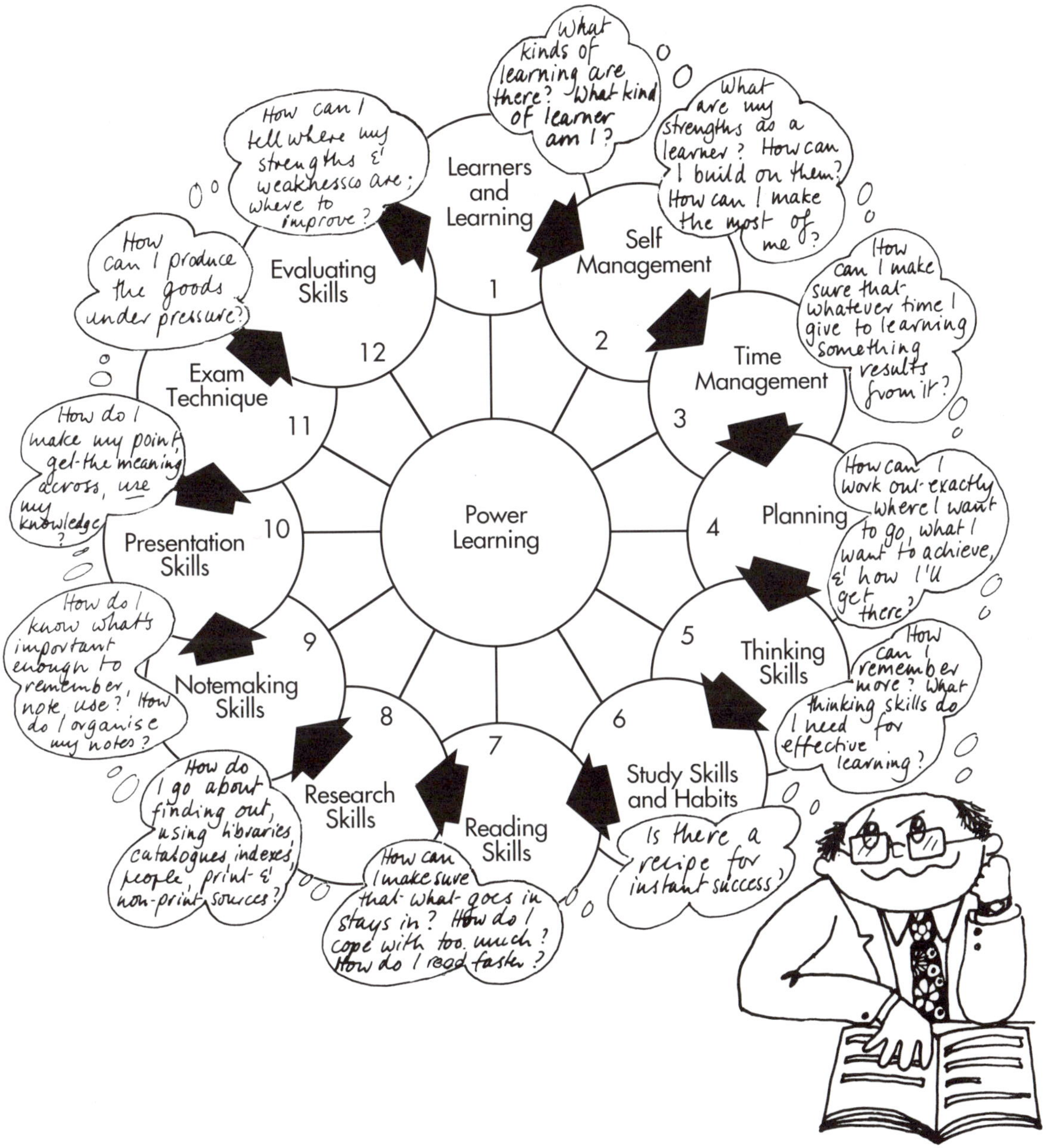

Each section has

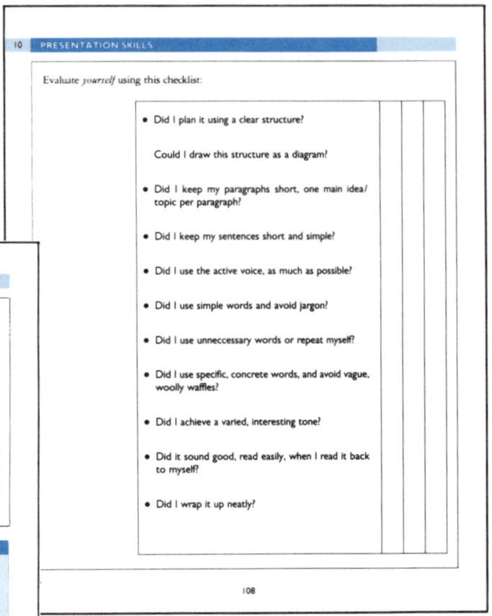

10 PRESENTATION SKILLS

Evaluate *yourself* using this checklist:

- Did I plan it using a clear structure?

  Could I draw this structure as a diagram?
- Did I keep my paragraphs short, one main idea/topic per paragraph?
- Did I keep my sentences short and simple?
- Did I use the active voice, as much as possible?
- Did I use simple words and avoid jargon?
- Did I use unneccessary words or repeat myself?
- Did I use specific, concrete words, and avoid vague, woolly waffles?
- Did I achieve a varied, interesting tone?
- Did it sound good, read easily, when I read it back to myself?
- Did I wrap it up neatly?

108

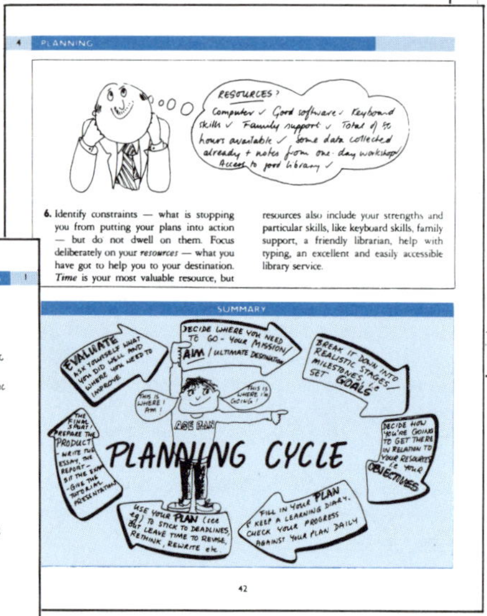

4 PLANNING

6. Identify constraints — what is stopping you from putting your plans into action — but do not dwell on them. Focus deliberately on your *resources* — what you have got to help you to your destination. *Time* is your most valuable resource, but resources also include your strengths and particular skills, like keyboard skills, family support, a friendly librarian, help with typing, an excellent and easily accessible library service.

SUMMARY

42

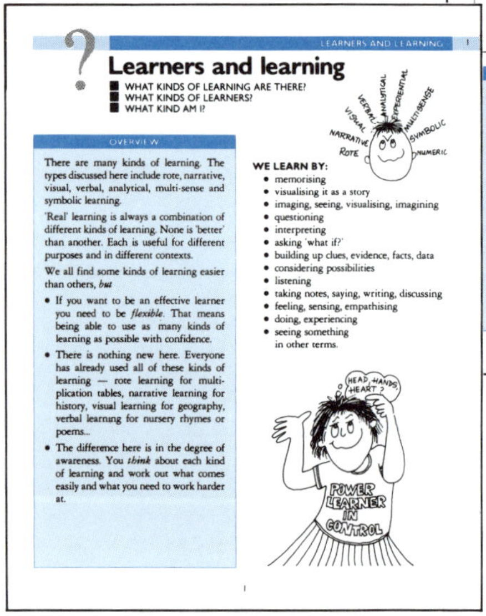

LEARNERS AND LEARNING 1

Learners and learning

- WHAT KINDS OF LEARNING ARE THERE?
- WHAT KINDS OF LEARNERS?
- WHAT KIND AM I?

OVERVIEW

There are many kinds of learning. The types discussed here include rote, narrative, visual, verbal, analytical, multi-sense and symbolic learning.

'Real' learning is always a combination of different kinds of learning. None is 'better' than another. Each is useful for different purposes and in different contexts.

We all find some kinds of learning easier than others, *but*

- If you want to be an effective learner you need to be *flexible*. That means being able to use as many kinds of learning as possible with confidence.
- There is nothing new here. Everyone has already used all of these kinds of learning — rote learning for multiplication tables, narrative learning for history, visual learning for geography, verbal learning for nursery rhymes or poems...
- The difference here is in the degree of awareness. You *think* about each kind of learning and work out what comes easily and what you need to work harder at.

WE LEARN BY:

- memorising
- visualising it as a story
- imaging, seeing, visualising, imagining
- questioning
- interpreting
- asking 'what if?'
- building up clues, evidence, facts, data
- considering possibilities
- listening
- taking notes, saying, writing, discussing
- feeling, sensing, empathising
- doing, experiencing
- seeing something in other terms.

1

- worksheets and templates where appropriate
- completed examples

- questionnaires
- practical advice
- examples
- diagrams
- summaries

- focus questions
- an overview
- a visual summary

Learners and learning

- WHAT KINDS OF LEARNING ARE THERE?
- WHAT KINDS OF LEARNERS?
- WHAT KIND AM I?

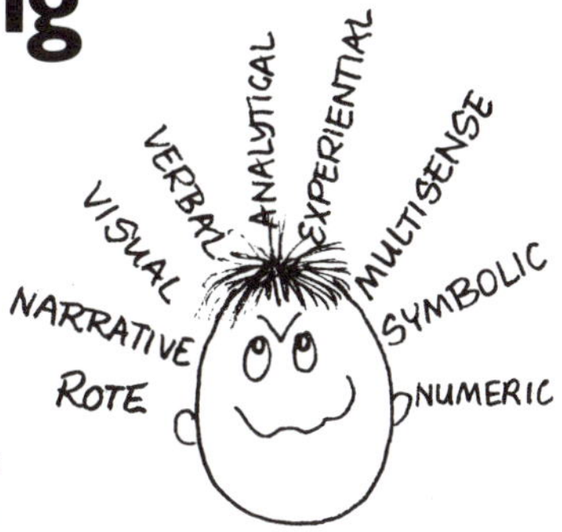

OVERVIEW

There are many kinds of learning. The types discussed here include rote, narrative, visual, verbal, analytical, multi-sense and symbolic learning.

'Real' learning is always a combination of different kinds of learning. None is 'better' than another. Each is useful for different purposes and in different contexts.

We all find some kinds of learning easier than others, *but*

- If you want to be an effective learner you need to be *flexible*. That means being able to use as many kinds of learning as possible with confidence.
- There is nothing new here. Everyone has already used all of these kinds of learning — rote learning for multiplication tables, narrative learning for history, visual learning for geography, verbal learning for nursery rhymes or poems...
- The difference here is in the degree of awareness. You *think* about each kind of learning and work out what comes easily and what you need to work harder at.

WE LEARN BY:

- memorising
- visualising it as a story
- imaging, seeing, visualising, imagining
- questioning
- interpreting
- asking 'what if?'
- building up clues, evidence, facts, data
- considering possibilities
- listening
- taking notes, saying, writing, discussing
- feeling, sensing, empathising
- doing, experiencing
- seeing something in other terms.

WHAT KINDS OF LEARNING ARE THERE?

ROTE LEARNING

All learning involves memory, but rote learning involves committing facts and figures to long-term memory. Rote learning can be:

- conscious (like saying times tables)

  or

- unconscious (like learning phone numbers without really trying). What you learn by rote, or 'by heart' can usually be triggered by stimuli like 7 x 8 = .

Some people find rote learning of figures easy, others difficult. Some people remember poems learned in childhood as long as they live. Others do not. Some people do appear to have better memories than others, but *you can train your mind to remember more.*

You will, to some extent, always remember what is important to you. Some people can remember their childhood phone number and their current one, but none in between. Can you remember your second to last phone number? If you did, did you use a trigger? Did you visualise the house and the phone with the number on its dial? Some people can remember better if they use triggers.

NARRATIVE LEARNING

This is probably best described as remembering in an 'and then' story-like sequence. This happened, then this happened, and then... You learn by seeing the facts as a story with a beginning, middle and end. Often the detail of this learning recedes to a few bald images — for the French Revolution it might be Marie Antoinette, the knitting women, and the guillotine — but it does not take long; a film, an article or a book can retrigger the narrative sequence of events.

Visual, emotional and deductive learning all play a part in narrative learning. It requires being able to imagine, and experience the feelings of the people involved and to see the causes which led to the effects.

Why were the aristocrats losing their heads as the workers knitted? Why couldn't they eat the cake recommended by Marie Antoinette? Who was she anyway? What happened to her, her husband, her children? Narrative learners enjoy seeing it like a video in their heads.

VISUAL LEARNING

At a practical level this is learning by looking and copying:

- being able to watch something and 'action replay' it in your head so that you can do it yourself.

At a cognitive level it is 'imagine if' learning:

- being able to see events in the mind's eye through visualising and imagining
- being able to 'see' the Mona Lisa
- being able to 'see' colour, shape, texture
- being able to conjure up the whole scene again, whether scenery, scenes from a film or from real-life experience, a painting or a sequence of movements.

Linked to lateral thinking, this ability to 'see' becomes the ability to visualise possibilities, alternatives or different futures and directions.

VERBAL LEARNING

Most learning is word-based. Whether stimuli and experiences come through sight, sound, touch or simply living, they become truly usable knowledge only when verbalised. Pre-verbal, half-grasped understanding is knowledge but it becomes more valuable when we can put it into words.

Words give shape to our world. They don't just describe reality, they shape and define it.

Different areas of learning have different languages, different terminologies and different jargon. If you learn the terminology, you unlock the concepts. Learners who have a feeling for the sound, sense and nuance of language have a learning tool that is much more powerful than the ability to learn words by heart. Words trigger precise associations, networks of understanding and knowledge.

ANALYTICAL LEARNING

Analytical learning is hypothetical and deductive. It is hypothetical in the sense of 'what if?', 'if this, then that'. It is deductive in the sense of 'so if', 'so if all these facts are true, then...'.

Analytical learning is a rich tool for:

- exploring possibilities
- looking at situations in terms of cause and effect
- collecting all the facts, evidence, data, opinion
- using this to confirm or reject an idea/hypothesis
- and coming up with answers, solutions, decisions, results.

Analytic reasoning puts a premium on logic. It is the stuff of detective stories, but also of a good research paper or thesis.

The facts or the evidence must support the conclusions. It's the stuff of Archimedes in the bathtub, the stuff of science, management, psychology, of human and environmental management, ecology, research and development.

MULTI-SENSE LEARNING

If the previous kinds of learning have been 'head' learning, this is 'hands and heart' learning.

It is

- when the foot seems to know independently of the head just how far and hard to kick the ball
- when the fingers reach instinctively for a letter on the keyboard
- when the body remembers a particular dance movement in response to a piece of music
- when driving becomes so automatic that you can reach your destination without consciously remembering changing gear, using the clutch, brakes, indicators in a synchronised sequence.

Computers and IT (information technology) emphasise the value of multi-sense learning. You need to understand both the logic of technology through your fingers, and the feeling dimension of automation — adapting technology to how people feel and act, not vice versa.

The feeling dimension of this learning is crucial, but often undervalued in an age of information overload. It is the instinctive, heart-driven ability

- to read the feelings of a meeting
- to read the feelings of an employer/ employee/colleague
- to sense the right thing to do or say in a situation.

It is often dealt with as 'communication skills' I think it is more useful to see it as *learning with the whole of you,* with all your senses.

It is worth spending time thinking through this concept of whole-person learning. Because head or cognitive learning is emphasised in the education system people often tend to think of this as 'real' learning. Children who like to learn by touch, by making and handling things, often grow up thinking they're 'dumb'.

Likewise, empathising and sensing are seldom valued as learning tools. Ironically, we now rely on management and communications courses to teach us to value the types of learning that school devalued !

SYMBOLIC AND NUMERIC LEARNING

This is probably the ultimate form of cognitive learning. It is the ability

- to see at an abstract level
- to see something in terms of something else, let x =, let this represent that...

Seeing something in terms of something else is at the heart of maths, physics, chemistry and, in fact, music. It is an enormously powerful cognitive tool.

Shunting symbols in the form of figures, equations and formulae somehow ends up being a spacecraft, a drug or a computer program of immense power. Statistics are a good example. They are symbols standing for various views of the world, often contradictory.

It is worth repeating the points made in the introduction:

- 'Real' learning is always a combination of different kinds of learning.
- We all find some kinds of learning easier than others.
- Everyone already uses all of these kinds of learning.
- None of these kinds of learning is better than any other although the education system has always valued 'head' over 'hands and heart' learning.
- To be an effective learner you need to be flexible. That means becoming comfortable with as many of these learning styles as you can.

Before you can do this, you need to work out what is your dominant or preferred learning style. This is your secret weapon as a learner. You know your strengths and limitations. You try to expand your learning repertoire and use it flexibly, but you avoid what unnerves and undermines you !

So, for example, I can marvel at and envy symbolic/numeric learning, but I simply cannot do it ! So I avoid what I can, suffer what I can't (like elementary statistics), and exploit the visual and verbal kinds of learning that come more easily. Most important, I don't see myself as 'dumb' just because I can't do maths.

However, as an educator, I often meet people who see themselves as dumb just because they didn't conform to school-based ideas of cleverness. They are intelligent, articulate, sensitive people who will always limit their own achievements by harbouring the illusion they are dumb.

Concentrate on working out your *strengths*, and building on them. Your limitations, and what you can do to compensate for them can come later. This checklist will help you.

CHECKLIST

		☺	☹
A	Do you find it easy to 'read' people and situations? Do you sometimes find yourself amazed at other people's insensitivity or lack of awareness of what's going on around them? Do you respond to things that feel right to you, that seem to strike a chord with you even though you can't really explain why?		
B	Do you find it easy to recall places, events, what someone was wearing, how a room was furnished? When you struggle to remember something, do you try to see it in your head? Do you find it easier to learn from well-laid out, well printed material than handwritten or photocopied notes?		

		☺	☹
C	Do you find it easy to remember stories? Do you enjoy listening to talks? Do you find it easier to remember if you read your notes aloud to yourself? Do you remember poems, quotes, names, relatively easily? Do you find that you haven't really grasped something until you've talked it back to yourself? Do you enjoy workshops and discussion groups where you can talk about what you do and share ideas? When asked to spell something, do you need to write it down?		
D	Do you find, especially as a child, you could remember things by heart relatively effortlessly. Are you the one the family turns to, to ask for a phone number? Do you annoy everyone by beating the panellists to the draw on TV quiz shows?		
E	Do you enjoy detective stories? Do you find it satisfying to find things out, get answers, build up all the bits and pieces until the picture becomes clear? Do you find not knowing something challenging? Or does it frighten and frustrate you not to be able to get an easy and immediate answer to something?		
F	Do you find maths and numeric work satisfying because it is so economical and clear cut, dispensing with all those difficult to pin down words? Do you get irritated with verbiage, with pages of thoughts and interpretations, preferring to see something reduced to a clear diagram or sequence of numbers that you feel able to come to grips with?		
G	Do you see yourself as a learning by doing sort of person? Do you find it difficult to do something if someone *tells* you how but relatively easy if someone *shows* you how? Similarly, do you prefer to show someone how to do something than to tell them, or write it down? Do you find that you can know something really well, but when you come to write it down you simply can't and you feel like a fool?		

It is unlikely that you answered 'yes' to all of these. If you answered 'yes' strongly to any of these, it will indicate your predominant, most comfortable and natural kind of learning.

A A strong 'yes' to A indicates that you are probably dominantly emotional/probably multi-sense in your approach to learning. To surge ahead you need to learn to combine these strengths with skills from the 'head' domain, and to concentrate on learning, listening, feeling *with your head* as well as your heart, your instinct and your hands.

B A strong 'yes' to B indicates a strongly visual approach to learning, which means you find visualising and conceptualising easier than most people because you can 'see' things clearly. You may find, though, that you get impatient with the detail and nitty-gritty of learning it to the point where you can regurgitate it. Strongly visual people often tend to be those who don't grasp the logic of numbers with the same clarity. But you may be an exception...

C Here a strong 'yes' was probably combined with a 'yes' for visual because verbal and visual strengths often complement one another. Alternatively it may well have been combined with A, emotional learning, because strongly verbal people often enjoy learning by discussion, by sharing views with other people. Strongly visual people, on the other hand, often tend to prefer reading things on their own. If you are in any doubt, ask yourself whether you'd prefer to learn something by going to a talk or reading about it. If you are strongly verbal, you fit into the biggest category of learners, but you can hone your visual and analytical skills to become a more powerful learner.

D Very few adult learners seem to claim rote learning as a predominant style, but many claim doing it with relative ease as a child. Although it is difficult for adults, you need to be able to use the techniques for learning occasions where there is no substitute.

E Predominantly analytic learners are actually quite rare! To become really powerful, they also need to activate heart-and-hands learning to pick up people clues as well as facts and figures.

F If you are adult and strongly symbolic/numeric in your preference, the world's your oyster *if* you realise that you are in a minority category and try consciously to see the world more like a verbal or visual learner. You need to value your colleagues and friends who are at home in the world of feelings and words.

G Strongly multi-sense, learning-by-doing people often avoid book learning because it feels uncomfortable. If you are one, you need to realise how much of your potential you could be wasting. One of the purposes of *Power Learning* is to make learning far more tangible and concrete, so you need to think of rolling up your sleeves and getting a grip on it!

WHAT KINDS OF LEARNERS ARE THERE?

Reading the previous section will have given you the opportunity to work out what types of learning you are better at and prefer. Each kind of learning is a complex of different *skills*. Asking which kinds of learning you find easier is really asking you what skills you already possess and use effectively. But there is more to learning than skills. The key factor that distinguishes one kind of learner from another is *attitude*. What is your attitude to learning? How do you approach it?

I have found it useful to divide the world into four basic types of learners although, obviously, nothing is that simple. Most people combine different types or shift from type to type depending on the topic, their degree of interest, or even the time of day and their state of mind. Still, it is worthwhile to ask yourself which of the four is your dominant/instinctive mode.

TYPES OF LEARNERS

THE BUILDER

likes systematic learning, building brick by brick on a solid foundation. Builders like to feel that each brick is in place before the next brick is put on top. Builders tend to be practical, factual, commonsense learners who enjoy learning by doing.

THE BAKER

is the opposite. Bakers like to see the whole cake in the mind's eye first. Bakers feel most comfortable when they can conceive of each part or ingredient in terms of what it contributes to the whole. Bakers tend to be visual, inventive, holistic, intuitive learners. They are driven as much by what feels right as what the book says is right.

THE BOFFIN

collects facts and figures, and delights in unrelated fragments of knowledge for knowledge's sake! Boffins are the Mastermind winners who like to know anything and everything. Unlike the Bakers, Boffins do not need to visualise the product before undertaking the process. Interesting things happen when Boffins learn to put these fragments of knowledge into a framework and analyse them.

THE BUTLER

also serves by standing and waiting ... Butlers are people who are content to wait and be told what to learn and what to do. They like others to tell them what they need to know and think. They prefer to know exactly where they stand. This does not mean that they lack intelligence or can't think for themselves. Far from it! They just find it easier to be given a direction than to make their own. We all like to be spoonfed at times, but Butlers are learners who, most of the time, prefer regurgitating what they know to deciding what they may need to know if no one tells them.

WHAT KIND OF LEARNER AM I?

I think I might be a *builder* because I'm definitely a learning-by-doing step-by-step type. I like systematic teachers — people who explain one step at a time and make sure you really understand before they go on.

I find it really difficult to talk in general terms and throw ideas and concepts around. It makes me feel insecure because I like to understand something fully, not just have some half-baked vague idea. I like concrete examples. I think I probably miss out on a lot because I tend to shut off and exclude things when they get a bit vague and waffly.

I think I'm a *baker* because I really like to get a global overview — I like to have a picture of the whole thing. I get really impatient if people start explaining something step-by-step, and I can't see what it's leading to. I'm not interested in Boffin-type detail. I'm not too hot at learning facts and figures and dates, and who did what to whom when and where. I prefer trying to work out *why* who did what to whom. If I understand why, I'm fine!

I should be more like a builder and try a more systematic approach to learning. I tend to flit around as long as *I* can see the whole picture. Other people find it difficult to follow me. I also tend to lose interest quickly when I've grasped something.

I think I'm a *boffin*. From childhood I've enjoyed knowing things. People often say I've got a good memory or excellent general knowledge. I don't know how I do it. It just seems to stick. It doesn't necessarily help me with exams and essays, though. Sometimes I think it's because I know a little about a lot, and successful study demands that you know a lot about a little!

I think I should build some baker skills because they seem to be able to see how things hang together better than I can. I probably need to invest in some glue to hang all my knowledge together, because I know I know it, but I don't always use what I know well!

I'm probably a *butler* most of the time because it was easy to get through school this way. If you waved your arm and volunteered answers and opinions you were a first-class wimp. Basically, if you kept your mouth shut you got along with everyone, and the teacher always told you what you needed to know in the end anyway.

I still find it easier if I know exactly what to do. Then you can just go and do it. I like things to be cut and dried. I don't like this guesswork stuff. Who says my opinion is right or wrong or better than someone else's? I prefer to stick to facts and leave it to someone else to do the interpreting!

Where do you fit in most of the time? It isn't cut and dried because you instinctively combine types of learning and change your approach depending on the learning task.

In the sections that follow some ideas will seem like common sense because they coincide with your existing view of learning. Some will not. They may feel artificial and uncomfortable. These are the ideas you should look at closely because they are the ones that will stretch you, your skills and attitudes.

SUMMARY

All of us have already practised every kind of learning, but as adults we have types and styles of learning we prefer and are better at. We all learn systematically (builders), holistically (bakers), factually (boffins) and by being directed (butlers), but we may be more comfortable in one or two modes. Effective learning means being aware of your strengths, weaknesses and preferences, and adding to your skills/ attitude repertoire.

Self-Management

- WHAT DO I NEED TO BE ABLE TO DO TO MANAGE MY LEARNING?
- HOW CAN I USE MY STRENGTHS AS A LEARNER AND EXPAND MY REPERTOIRE OF LEARNING STRATEGIES?

OVERVIEW

If you read the cartoon caption and recognise yourself with a sinking feeling, take heart — you're *normal*.

Many books on study skills talk about how to improve concentration, motivation, retention and recall without acknowledging the reassuring fundamental truth.

We *all* dream, doodle, dawdle, delude and make a habit of procrastination and self-deception when we need to study or write. It is part of the human condition. If you do anything else you are *abnormal.*

However, if you want to succeed as a learner you have to learn to do unnatural things. After all, is sliding down a slope with bits of wood strapped to your feet natural? Likewise, learning to manage yourself as a learner may feel unnatural and uncomfortable in the short term.

This section looks at seven strategies that underpin effective learning. It directs you to where they are dealt with in more depth in this book. There is a questionnaire to help you diagnose your self-management strengths and limitations.

The essence of self-management in learning is to be able to assess your own performance by asking yourself objective questions and responding to the answers without making excuses or blaming anyone or anything.

WHAT DO I NEED TO DO TO BE ABLE TO MANAGE MY LEARNING?

Being able to manage yourself as a learner is the key to getting the best out of yourself and making the best use of your strengths. You can know all about calories, kilojoules, carbohydrates and fibre, but to lose weight you actually need to manage your eating! Similarly you need to manage your learning.

There are seven useful strategies for managing your learning. This section introduces them briefly, and they are all followed up in later sections. The point to take here is that you need all seven:

- to manage your learning effectively
- to feel that you are in control of your learning
- to feel that you have an organisational framework into which you harness your learning strengths.

LEARNING DIARY

1. There is only one way to get total control over your learning. That is to *use ways of seeing yourself objectively as a learner*, charting and evaluating your own progress.

You need a *learning diary*. This is a notebook where you set out your learning targets, and where you record each day, in the briefest possible way, what you have done and whether you have met your self-set targets. This is an example of one completed page. The template, which you can copy or photocopy, is on page 21.

<u>Example</u>

Use the blank page facing the diary page to record comments about the content of the task.

Using a cheap, lined exercise book is fine. You'll soon adapt the format to suit your own needs, but *always* keep these elements: objectives/ time planned/ what you actually did.

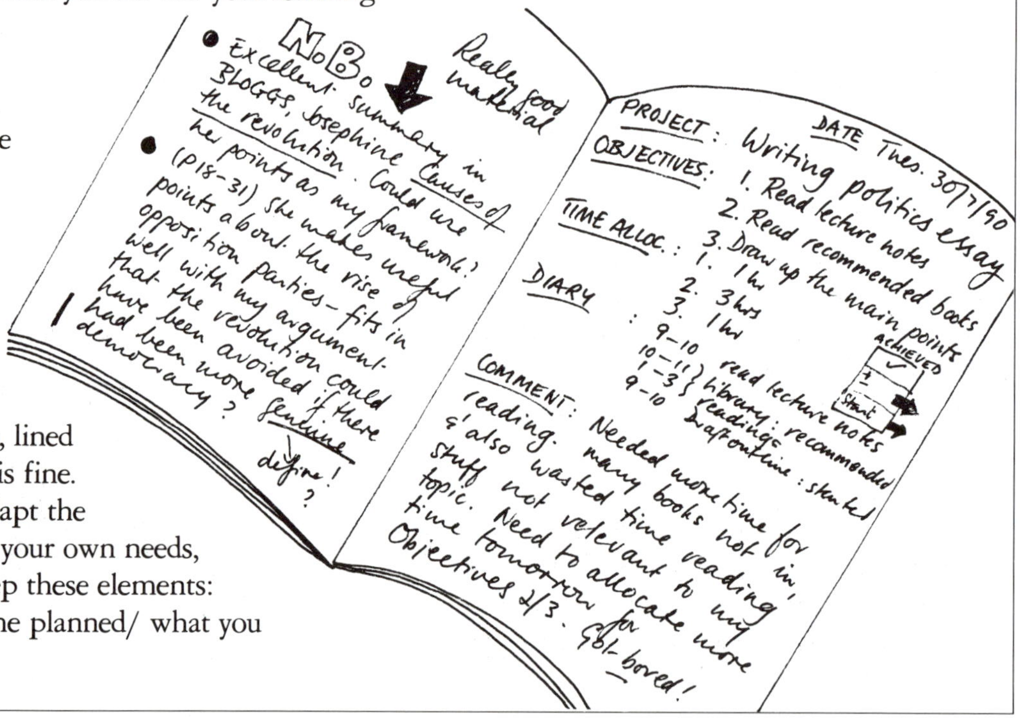

TIME MANAGEMENT

2. You need to be able to *manage your time* (see Section 3). This means doing as *little* study/reading/writing as you can to achieve what you need to. It does *not* mean punishing yourself by never doing anything else. It means employing conscious time management techniques and being honest with yourself in using the results to improve your own performance. The key concept is minimum input (of time) for maximum output (in terms of results and achievements)!

PLANNING

3. You need to be able to *plan* — to set your own targets which are realistic and achievable (see Section 4). There is no point in having a big beautiful dream (like getting an A, finishing a thesis, getting a first-class pass) unless you can set yourself directions for getting there. You also need more precise week-by-week and day-by-day ways and means for getting there.

THINKING SKILLS

4. You need to sharpen the blades of your mind as a tool — training your memory, training yourself to use lateral thinking techniques and other *thinking skill equivalents of muscle stretching*! You need to do your daily dozen mental toe touches and knee bends if you want to develop mental suppleness and stamina. It does not happen automatically any more than it does with physical fitness. Mind-stretching routines and recipes are given throughout the book, but particularly in Sections 5, 6, 7, 8 and 9.

COMMUNICATIONS

5. You need to learn the trick of *seeing study and research as communication* — a conversation, a dialogue with others. If they cannot understand, you have not succeeded. This is easy to say, but more difficult to do. You need to constantly ask 'Why?', 'Why am I doing this?', 'For whom?', 'What do they expect/need?' (Section 10). You need to build up a portfolio of examples of good essays, papers, exam questions or reports.

PERFORMING

6. You need to treat exams as opportunities, not bogeys! *Everyone* hates them, but anyone can learn to use them as a platform for showing off what they know. You don't like showing off? *Everyone* enjoys showing off something they can do well! The secret of exams is to see them not as alien and hostile forces 'out there' ready to expose and humiliate you, but as a well-disposed audience ready to applaud a skilled performance. And if you apply your learning and revision skills systematically and consciously, your performance *will* be skilled (see Section 11).

SELF-EVALUATION

7. You need to get into the habit of being your own judge. You do not leave it to examiners to judge you. That gives them too much power! At best they exist to comment on your own judgement of yourself. It is not enough to discipline yourself to study so many hours a day, to read so many books, write so many pages. You need to stop and take time to ask yourself:

- 'How well am I doing? What have I actually achieved?'
- 'From the main points I've listed, could I rough out an exam answer?'
- 'Am I using my visual strengths by concentrating on seeing it as a story?'
- 'Were my targets realistic? Did I leave myself enough time to rewrite it?'

Writing the answers down in your *Learning Diary* may seem like a waste of time, but it is a key self-evaluation strategy (see Section 12).

■ HOW CAN I USE MY STRENGTHS AS A LEARNER AND EXPAND MY REPERTOIRE OF LEARNING STRATEGIES?

Section 1 will have given you some idea of what kind of learner you are and your natural learning strengths and aptitudes. But you can *be* quite good at learning and still not *do* it very well. This is where self-management comes in. Whatever you are good at, it still needs to be managed.

When you talk to adults who didn't see themselves as spectacular successes at school, they always claim, in the most general terms, that they weren't good at 'that sort of thing', they lacked 'self-discipline', they 'couldn't write'. This may be true up to a point, but it isn't particularly helpful.

To start managing your own learning you need to be two things:

1. *honest* with yourself

2. *specific* about your shortcomings.

To help you to do this, there is a questionnaire which highlights problems that are common to most learners. There are strategies and techniques sprinkled throughout the book which will help you to manage aspects of your learning. But the more specific you can be about where you *know* you struggle, the better.

To make it specific, try to think of an instance, or several, in the past where you feel you under-performed, let yourself down. Replay it in your head. 'See' the situation. Try to remember exactly what you felt. Did you work out, at the time, exactly what went wrong? Or did you just feel furious with yourself and the world?

Remember that success is *relative*. *Everyone* has experienced lack of success at some stage. This exercise benefits anyone and everyone for this reason.

QUESTIONNAIRE: COMMON LEARNING PROBLEMS	
1. You just can't remember enough?	Section 5
2. You just can't seem to get the main points, whatever is wanted?	Section 5, 7, 8, 9
3. You just can't focus — your mind is a great fuzz of irrelevant rubbish and you can't seem to focus it for exams, or essays, or anything?	Section 11
4. You work and work, and nothing seems to stick?	Section 9
5. You read and read and it all ends up as sludge inside your head?	Section 7 - 10
6. You find it difficult to find the information in the first place?	Section 8
7. You find it difficult to sift through too much information and know what is important?	Section 8, 9
8. It is all in your head but you can't seem to get it down on paper?	Section 10
9. You start with good intentions but end up doing it all at the last moment?	Section 3, 4, 11
10. You take notes and all that, but end up with a wad of notes and photocopies that take almost as much time to sort through as the original?	Section 9
11. You studied all your notes, but you still didn't do well in the exam?	Section 11
12. You feel sure that some people just have a knack, and you aren't one of them?	Section 2, 12

If you answer 'yes' to most of these, it means you are normal! No one ever totally conquers the feeling of not knowing enough, not being able to express it clearly enough.

The point of self-management is not to deny what you feel, but to get it under control. Telling people the solutions to their problems seldom works. The essence of *self*-management is learning to judge yourself. To do this you need to ask yourself quite specific questions.

Knowing that you have a particular problem is fine, but the first step in solving it is to learn to turn it into specific questions. Try to relate the questions below to the problems on the previous page. Some of the questions may relate to more that one problem. The aim is not to trick you, but to give you practice in turning problems into questions.

A 'OK, so what is this author really saying? Can I write it down to clarify it?'

B 'I'm finding this really hard. Why? What haven't I done? What else should I do?'

C 'What are the main things I'm trying to say?'

D 'Have I backed them with good examples, verifiable data?'

E 'Is this what my audience expects to be told/expects me to know?'

F 'Have I got the main things down? Is the structure clear? Does it read OK?'

G 'Can I shut my book and jot down the main points?'

H 'So what did I achieve in the last hour? What could I have done to make the time I spent more productive?'

I 'Have I got a plan, a structure before I start to write?'

J 'So what questions do I need to get answered before I start reading?'

K 'What's my final deadline? What do I need to do? Can I break it down into stages and work out how long each stage will take?'

L 'Can I read less by focusing my reading round my key questions?'

A 5
B 12
C 2 or 3 or 7
D 6
E 3 or 2
F 11
G 1
H 4
I 8
J 10
K 9
L 7

You will only learn to manage your learning to full effect if you can see yourself clearly as a person. The learning you is not a different person. How you approach learning will reflect the whole you, who and what you are as a person. It helps to think about your 'internal community', as John Mulligan* calls it in *The Personal Management Handbook*. This is all the different 'yous' that make up the whole you — the different roles you play, the different needs you have in each of these roles.

The essence of keeping yourself happy and healthy is to maintain a balance between the members of this internal community. It may be useful to give them labels as Mulligan does, like 'Creative Genius' or 'Destructive Saboteur'. If you can distance yourself sufficiently you may be able to work out which of your internal characters is making your learning difficult, which you need to be more aware of and which you need to get under firmer control. You may find that your self-concept of 'Dopey Idiot' is being replaced by 'Slow Pacer', 'Steady Achiever' or 'Realistic Planner'.

Can you integrate your student/learner character into your total character cast? Photocopy this exercise, complete it and stick it into your *Learning Diary* once a month. Don't look at your previous attempt. Tick the characteristics that apply to you; cross out those that don't. Fill in the gaps to describe yourself as a learner. Check back over your forms every few months to see whether your self-concept as a learner has improved.

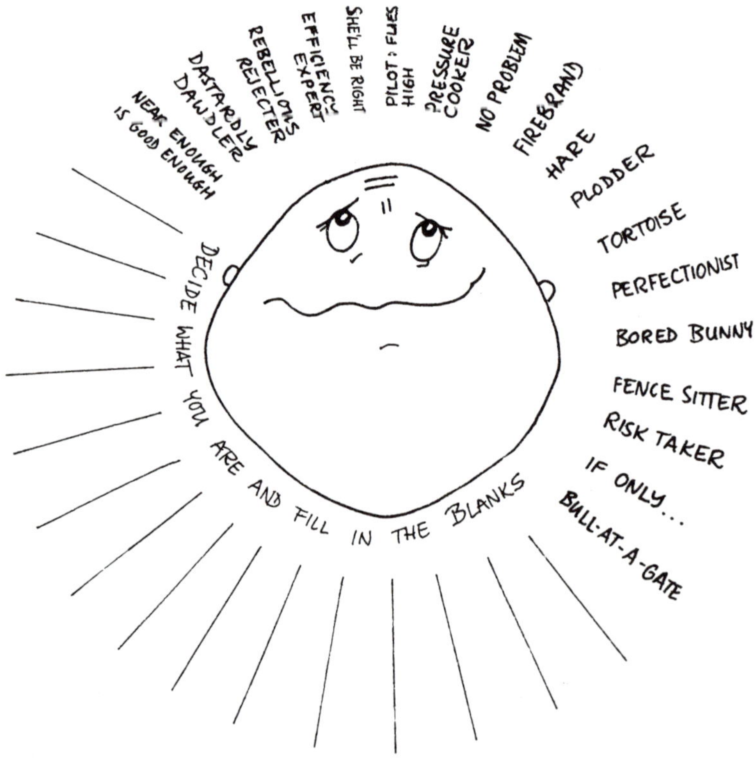

*Mulligan, John (ed) *The Personal Management Handbook : How to make the most of your potential*, London: Sphere, 1988.

LEARNING DIARY : TEMPLATE

DATE: PROJECT: OBJECTIVES: achieved? 1. .... 2. .... 3. .... 4. .... 5. .... 6.	List objectives for the day in order of priority. Tick if achieved at the end of the day. If not, mark with a bold arrow to carry over (see example).
TIME ALLOCATED: Total:	Be *realistic*! Decide how many hours you can afford, and what you will do in that time.
DIARY:	Record what you actually did, hour by hour.
COMMENT:	Comments on what you actually achieved, what you were pleased with, what gave you problems, i.e. your performance.

Time Management

■ HOW CAN I ENSURE THAT WHATEVER TIME I GIVE TO LEARNING, SOMETHING RESULTS FROM IT?

OVERVIEW

Rich, poor, in sickness or in health, we all have one thing in common — 24 hours a day!

What makes us different is how effectively we use these 24 hours. Some people may be naturally better at using time than others, just as some people naturally need more or less sleep, have more or less energy.

Learning to manage time is not something restricted to executives on fancy courses! It's something that everyone needs — you control time or time controls you.

The 10 time management techniques described here are simple. What is difficult is putting them into practice — not because they are hard but because they are unbelievably tedious, require an enormous amount of self-discipline and persistence, and because you don't see any immediate result.

Months after you begin using time management techniques consciously and continuously, you will look back and say, 'I'm managing my time much better now'. But if you rest on your laurels and stop using the time management techniques, you'll find that you slip behind again.

Time management is a boring but totally unavoidable chore! There are no short cuts. You need to make time management part of your life, like brushing your teeth!

Time management, as the last section explained, is a key dimension of self-management. What follows is a step-by-step guide to effective time management. Many people find this daunting and intimidating. This is silly because you really need to see time management in perspective. Like self-management, time management is not optional. You can't *not* do it. You can't opt out and stop time! We all manage our time constantly anyway.

It is impossible to have lived a normal life without using the techniques of time management, even if you weren't aware that this is what they were! If you have got to places on time, caught buses and trains, met friends, or planned a day to combine a job, sport, a party, a film, whatever, you've used time management. So, the first thing to understand about time management is that it is a way of structuring and formalising what we all do anyway.

Like much of this book, this section will put into words and consolidate what you do already. It will help you to understand the apparent contradiction in time management. When you first start using conscious time management techniques it can feel like an intolerable restriction on your freedom, like living in self-made shackles. But when you get used to it, when the processes become automatic and unconscious, it actually has the effect of liberating you, setting you free from the 24-hour prison.

The 10 time management techniques described in this section deal with time management in general. Techniques for making more effective use of your study/learning time are incorporated into the subsequent sections that focus on aspects of learning. Section 9, for instance, discusses ways of sorting and filing your notes for easy retrieval and use. In Section 7 we look at ways of getting maximum benefit from your reading time. Section 6, which deals with study skills and habits should be read in conjunction with this section, because managing your time is probably the key to effective studying.

Time management is something that you can only learn by *doing*. You can't learn it by reading about it. The first step is to work out your present strengths and limitations. The questionnaire on page 25 will help you.

Time management is like brushing your teeth — you feel virtuous if you do it, and if you do not you feel mildly dishonest and dirty!

ASSESS YOUR TIME MANAGEMENT SKILLS

1. Are you the sort of person who likes to plan ahead? Do you like to know what is happening, what you're doing when and where?

2. Do you write lists of what you need to do — on bits of paper, in a diary, on your calendar? Do you get a sense of satisfaction when you tick off the things you have done?

3. Do you enjoy routine? Do you find life easier if you can anticipate that certain things will happen in certain ways at certain times?

4. Do you like to work at a fairly even pace, with fairly regular hours and moderate pressure?

5. Do you like to relax and let life happen? Do you prefer to respond to life as it happens rather than planning too far ahead and tying it all up neatly?

6. Do you procrastinate? Do you have good intentions but somehow end up doing everything at the last minute, and quite enjoying it?

7. Do you pride yourself in working well under pressure, when there's a deadline?

8. Do you leave your income tax and paying bills to the last possible moment even when you have the money because you just can't be bothered?

9. Do you enjoy variety, working in spurts and relaxing totally in between?

10. Do you get a buzz out of crises? Do you like coping with whatever happens when it happens? Do you find yourself amazed when other people seem to go to pieces and get angry and upset when things go wrong?

You don't need to be a genius to work out that if you answered 'yes' to the first four questions, time management will come more naturally to you because that's the way you are anyway! It will consolidate for you the fact that organising your time is just a natural extension of organising your life.

If you answered 'yes' to questions 5-10, relax! You're in the majority, not the minority, and you're probably easier to live with than the walking clock type! *But* you'll never learn to realise your full potential until you train yourself to do the opposite *when you want to* and *when you need to.*

If you only feel comfortable in formal clothes you will lose out on a lot of the joys of living. If you are proud of the fact that you only ever wear informal clothes, the same applies. The ideal situation is the right clothes for the right occasion. Think of time management as like *climbing into a set of clothes*, climbing into a way of behaving and organising yourself. Whatever your type, *do* the practical workout!

■ PUTTING TIME MANAGEMENT TO WORK: LEARNING BY DOING

START by keeping a 24-hour diary for two or three days. Except when you are actually asleep, write down each hour what you have done. (See template p. 34.)

1. At the end of your two to three days, average the time you have spent doing regular activities, sleeping, eating, working, attending college, relaxing with family and friends, playing sports, gardening, travelling, shopping, doing housework, etc.

   Starting with the 24-hour total, subtract the average time you spend on each of these regular activities. How many hours do you have left?

   This is your *discretionary time* and, presumably, what you will use for independent study, whether you are studying fulltime or part-time.

   However you shunt the figures around, there will be *appallingly little discretionary time* left. And what you haven't done yet is to add up and subtract average time for contingencies and emergencies — taking the car to the garage, the cat to the vet, going to the dentist, doctor, hairdresser, etc, etc. It's a salutary and utterly depressing exercise *for everyone!*

2. There is only one answer. Try to reduce what you spend on regular activities by taking short cuts and doing things faster, so that you can expand your discretionary time. Even the act of *working out your discretionary/study time every day* is a positive time management step, because you will find yourself less inclined to waste it when you realise what a precious commodity discretionary time is!

Accept that this is *unnatural* and feels revolting at first. No one likes to live by the clock. We all love to dawdle and waste time, but let this become a treat, not a way of life. Give yourself one day a week or fortnight when you treat yourself to a day of mucking around, dawdling and flitting aimlessly from one unfinished thing to another, being a total slob, a blob, a vegetable!

3. For the rest of the time, do the opposite.

- *Keep a strict time planner* (see p. 33).
- Force yourself to fill it in as you go, at least every half-hour.
- Look back at the end of each day and ask yourself:

- □ whether you accomplished all the major objectives you set yourself
- □ if not, why not? Did you set too many? Were they unrealistic?
- □ whether you paced yourself and rationed your energy by working in short intensive bursts, alternating demanding and intensive tasks with relatively effortless and mundane tasks
- □ whether you did one huge spurt and then flopped around exhausted for the rest of the day
- □ whether you shuffled paper around from one pile to another, or got on with sorting, discarding and filing it
- □ whether you had lots of five-minute breaks
- □ whether you had lots of five-minute breaks that became 25-minute breaks!
- □ whether you remembered that you had a body attached to your neck, and fed and watered it and gave it a break, some exercise and some air when it sent you signals
- □ whether you jumped around from task to task accomplishing little, or whether, allowing for inevitable minor distractions, you managed to concentrate and get one or two major tasks finished.

- Look back through your time sheets at the end of, say, a week and compile a list of time wasters — the things that regularly distract you and get you off task and target.
- At the end of, say, a month check your time sheets against your list of time wasters. Are the same things coming up again and again? If so, you know what you need to tackle. It may well be excessively long phone interruptions. It may be family/domestic interrruptions that could be avoided. It may well be your own work patterns — putting in the time but delaying getting down to it.

These time sheets are the most important, but also the most tedious part of time management, and the part that people abandon first. Don't, because they provide the data from which you diagnose and remedy your own time management problems.

4. *Train yourself to use your brain while your hands and body are doing mundane things,* like ironing, mowing the lawn or walking to the bus stop. It requires a massive effort of will, but it does work.

Try to recall, as you walk to work, the main points in yesterday's lecture or the main arguments in the book you have just read. Try to imagine it as a dialogue in your own head: 'If someone asked me to tell them the main reasons for the Marsh Arabs' way of life, what would I say?' Then say it in your head as you might to them. It comes as quite a shock to realise how little you can articulate when you thought, in fact, that you had understood and remembered quite a lot.

It is particularly effective to use this as an exam revision technique, using previous exam questions as the starting point. Not only is this a time economy, given that you are doing two things at once, but it encourages you to firm up your ideas about what and how to work in the time you have allocated for formal study.

HYDROTHERAPY!

5. However, you also need to *learn to switch off completely*, to clear your mind and focus on something completely different. Most of us have less difficulty doing this than doing two things at once! If you think of your mind as an appliance with batteries that run dry if you leave the appliance on too long, you need to work out what recharges you and do it *regularly*.

With some people it is exercise. With others it is soaking in a bath.

Some like to get away from it all — solitary walks and beautiful scenery. Others like pubs and crowds and noise. No problem! The only problem with switching off tends to be switching on again. This is why, like any other activity, you need to set a strict time limit and stick to it!

6. Assuming that you have now done the time diary exercise (1), worked out your average and daily discretionary time (2), started to log what you do all day and every day using time sheets (3), begun to train yourself to use the mental space created by mundane, physical chores (4), and learned to switch off and regenerate (5), you should be starting to see a pattern emerge.

Consolidate what you are learning about your own use of time by *completing your Learning Diary every night* (see p. 21).

In other words, there are two things to complete : your daily time planning sheets (3) and your Learning Diary. Use the comment section and be *positive*. By all means say what you did not accomplish, but focus on what you *did* accomplish. Jot down briefly anything you finished, anything you know now that you didn't know yesterday. Focus on what you did well/better. Don't use it as an opportunity for self-criticism.

The difference between the daily time planning sheets and the Learning Diary is that the time planning sheets cover your whole day and everything you do, the aim being to squeeze as much discretionary/study time as possible out of each day, and to make use of thinking time/mental space throughout the day.

The Learning Diary is just a record of your learning and your development as a learner. The emphasis in both is *brevity*. You fill in your time sheets as you go along, *not at the end of the day*. You fill in your learning diary at the end of the day, taking no more than 10 minutes.

7. When you have finished something, achieved an objective, done something you could not do previously, *treat yourself*. It might be a mindless hour in front of TV, an hour in the garden, a cup of fresh coffee, a long soak in the bath, an extra chapter of the novel you are reading — anything *you* value.

On the other hand, if you fail to reach what should have been an easily achievable target, and it was your problem — you got distracted, shuffled paper, stroked the cat, whatever — force yourself to catch up the next day.

It sounds Calvinistic, but if you work a time credit/debit system and you find yourself constantly owing yourself study/learning time that you have frittered away on other things, it does tend to make you more conscious of making good use of whatever time you spend learning.

The psychology is the same as working out your discretionary time and keeping a time log. The very act of doing it is a positive time management technique because it makes you more conscious of what you actually do with your time.

8. Whatever you do, however pressured you are, try to get regular exercise and relaxation. If exercise is your relaxation, that is excellent — two for the price of one. But even if your relaxation is sedentary — watching TV, doing patchwork, fixing things, collecting stamps — you still need regular exercise, so walk to work/college/university/the shops, and walk upstairs instead of taking the lift.

If all else fails, get an aerobic rebounder (not a cheap mini-trampoline) and even if you cannot persuade yourself to see it as a treat, it will become a habit. At very least, learn to do deep breathing and a few simple stretches and do them regularly!

9. With only 24 hours in the day it seems a waste to spend up to eight of them asleep! An essential part of time management is to get as much benefit as you can from the time you spend sleeping. If you go to bed stiff with tension and with your mind still racing, you will probably sleep, but get questionable benefit from your sleep. Sleep is obviously affected by your state of mind, but several things can help to ensure that you benefit fully from your sleep:

- Regular exercise during the day.
- Doing yoga breathing (deep, from the diaphragm) and relaxation before you go to sleep.
- Avoiding coffee at night and instead drink herbal tea.
- Drinking hot milk before bed.
- Deciding what you will dream, i.e. running pleasant and positive thoughts through your mind before you drop off. You won't dream precisely that, but it does seem to lead to more positive and restful sleep when you are stressed.

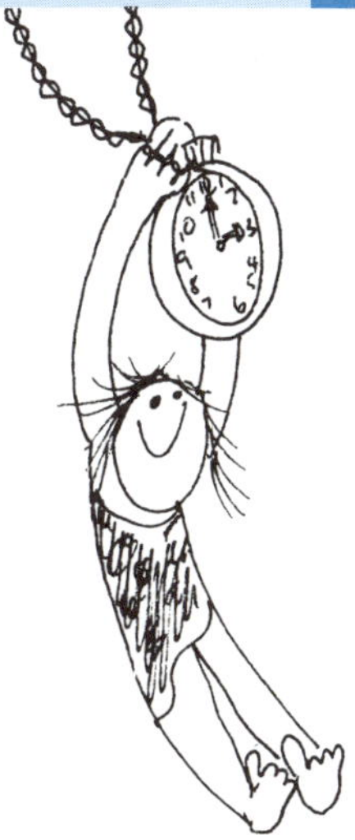

- 'You are what you eat' is a truism precisely because it is true. Lots of fresh fruit and veg, and avoiding rich, fatty, spicy foods, especially at night, does pay long-term dividends.

  You may find that:

- You end up needing less sleep (whoopee, more discretionary time!).
- You feel better when you wake — have more energy during the day.

10. Do a proper stocktake at regular intervals. Once a month is a good idea. Look back at your time planning sheets and your Learning Diary.

- Are you getting more done?
- Are you planning your time better?
- Are you setting realistic objectives?
- Are you overcoming your worst time wasters, or dealing with them even marginally better, like shorter phone conversations?
- Are you pleased with yourself and your use of time overall?
- Do you feel reasonably well, happy, energetic?
- Or are you more of a stressed, burnt-out wreck than when you started time management? If so, what does this tell you about yourself?
- Are you getting rest and relaxation, and exercise, every day?
- Do you change pace at weekends, or at least one day a week?

Overleaf you will find the template you need to do this time management workout. When it becomes a natural part of your routine you can build it into your diary, as shown below. The reason people often give for not doing time management is that they can't afford the time! This doesn't wash!

Time management *does* take some time when you first start because it involves writing down and thinking about things you haven't done before. It also involves looking at your whole day. What this example shows you, is that when you have integrated the techniques you can decide when to apply them. You can *choose* to manage your time only during the working day, five days a week. The point is to learn to use the techniques so that *you* can choose when to use them, or not.

EXAMPLE

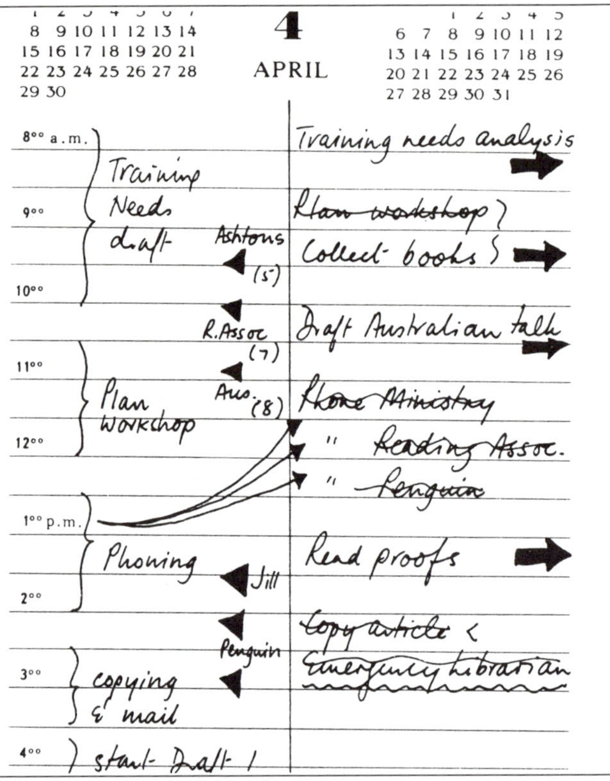

A useful method is to draw a line dividing the page in half. The right half is for what you plan to do. The left half is for what you actually do. As you accomplish the objectives you set yourself, cross them off. A highlighter pen is useful. This makes it easy to see what remains unfinished at the end of the day. Arrows (in a different colour) show what must be carried over to the next day.

If you find it helpful, total the amount of time you spent on study, or even, on a bad day, on unavoidable interruptions. At the end of the month stocktake this provides the data for your analysis.

SUMMARY

Time management is something that everyone does already. The advantage of formalising it into a set of techniques lies in making you more conscious of how you use your time, and how you can achieve more with the 24 hours we all have in one day! The techniques covered here include:

1. Monitoring your regular activities for a few days.
2. Working out your free/discretionary time for study.
3. Keeping daily time planning sheets; working out avoidable time wasters.
4. Training yourself to use free mental space while your hands are busy.
5. Learning to switch off and recharge your mental batteries.
7. Rewarding yourself with treats when you achieve your targets.
8. Getting regular exercise and relaxation.
9. Making the most of the time you spend sleeping.
10. Stocktaking at regular intervals — assessing your time management.

TIME PLANNER TEMPLATE

Day, date: ....

Things to do today (Main things)		Priority order	Other things to do today (bits and pieces)
	1.		
	2.		
	3.		
	4.		
	5.		
	6.		

What I actually did:	Interruptions: avoidable/unavoidable	Comment:
6.00		
6.30		
7.00		
7.30		
8.00		
8.30		
9.00		
9.30		
10.00		
10.30		
11.00		
11.30		
12.00		
12.30		
1.00		
1.30		
2.00		
2.30		
3.00		
3.30		
4.00		
4.30		
5.00		
5.30		
6.00		
6.30		
7.00		
7.30		
8.00		
8.30		
9.00		
9.30		
10.00		
10.30		

24 HOUR DIARY

am/pm	24-hour	What I did during each hour?
6 am	0600 hrs	
7	0700	
8	0800	
9	0900	
10	1000	
11	1100	
12	1200	
1pm	1300	
2	1400	
3	1500	
4	1600	
5	1700	
6	1800	
7	1900	
8	2000	
9	2100	
10	2200	
11	2300	
12	2400	
1am	0100	
2	0200	
3	0300	
4	0400	
5am	0500	

Planning

■ HOW CAN I WORK OUT EXACTLY WHERE I WANT TO GO, WHAT I WANT TO ACHIEVE, AND HOW I'M GOING TO GET THERE?

OVERVIEW

The management guru, Drucker, popularised the saying that if you don't know where you're going, how will you know when you get there, or words to that effect.

Knowing where you are, where you want to be and working out how to get there, and how your journey went when you reach your destination, are the essence of planning.

Whether you are planning a career, a month, an essay or a research project, you need to start from your ultimate destination or *aim,* and work backwards from there asking:

- What do I ultimately want to achieve?
- How much time have I got?
- What resources have I got?
- Who will help me?
- So, how, when and where will I do it?

Planning and time management are closely related. Time management is generally applied to managing time on a day-to-day basis. Planning works to a long-term frame, weeks, months or several years. Planning, if you like, is where you are going. Time management is one of the ways you use to get there.

There are many types of planning. Probably the most useful for learners are *strategic* (setting broad directions) and *tactical* (translating these directions into short-term plans). These techniques have been simplified and adapted for study applications in this section. It starts with six essential elements of planning, helps you to set objectives, and then, acknowledging that the most significant constraint in planning is *yourself*, suggests personal planning strategies and includes some planning templates and examples.

HOW CAN I WORK OUT EXACTLY WHERE I WANT TO GO?

1. Planning, like learning, self-management and time management, is something we all do all the time anyway. However, it really becomes powerful when you learn to focus on it consciously, when you learn to *write your plans down* and use them as signposts to monitor your own progress.

2. *Planning is not inflexible.* You revise your planning continuously. It may well be a sign of strength, not weakness, if you change and adapt your objectives as you go along. What you try to do less often is to change your *main direction.* This can become emotionally and physically exhausting, as anyone who has changed careers can attest. There may well, however, be times when it is the best thing to do.

The main point is to see plans as infinitely adjustable and flexible. They are not whalebone corsets! Many people think that once they have a plan, they must adhere to it letter by letter. Not so! A plan is a starting point. It gives a sense of direction and provides signposts along the way to help you decide how far you have come and how well you are doing.

3. *Planning is horribly difficult to get right!* Most people plan to do too much. The rule of thumb is: plan, then cut the amount in half and give yourself twice as long as you thought you'd need!

Talking about realistic planning and *doing* it is something else again. Making planning work for you is really only something you can teach yourself.

An effective self-teaching method is always to plan with your *previous* plan in front of you. Which of your goals did you not reach? Why not? Which of the problems were *extrinsic* (external, beyond your control, imposed on you)? Which were *intrinsic* (related to you, your self-set goals and objectives, your lack of management skills)? Are you going to repeat the same mistakes?

By working with *evidence* of your planning in front of you, you can see more clearly what *is* your problem and can be dealt with, and what is inevitable — the reason why planning can only ever be open-ended and speculative, never a blueprint.

4. Planning involves setting broad directions, signposts along the way and ways and means of getting there. In strategic management terminology these are called:

the *mission* statement (overall aim or direction)
the *goals* (more specific directions or signposts)
the *objectives* (the detailed routemap, with realistic, achievable targets and deadlines).

For our purposes we will use the terms *aim, goals, objectives*. You will also need *strategies* (exactly how you are going to get there — bus, boat or roller skates). This is where *strategic* (long-term) planning becomes *tactical* (short-term) planning. As long as you know where you are going (aim, goals and objectives), you can afford to be flexible in how you are going to get there.

This is a useful diagram to anchor the planning process in your mind:

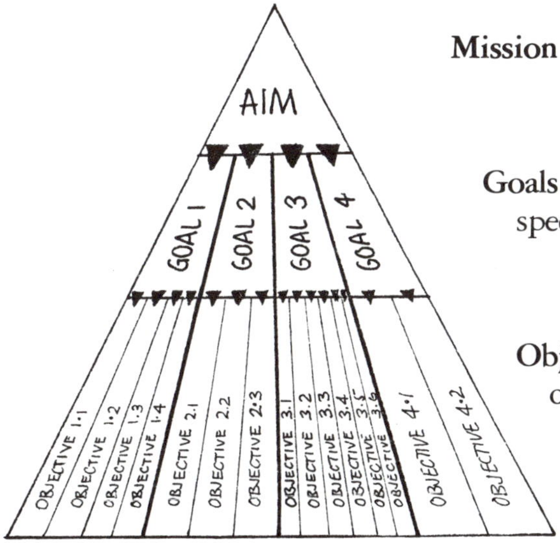

Mission or Aim : Where am I going (broadly)?

Goals relating to mission : Where am I going (more specifically)?

Objectives : Each goal translates into any number of specific, concrete, achievable objectives which represent signposts.

<u>Example</u>
If you are working on an essay or research project (your *aim*,) and one of your *goals* is to complete your research by 25 April, your *objective* may be to collect all your material and data by 5 April. Then you discover that some of the books are out on loan.
Does this invalidate your *aim*, your *goals*, or this particular *objective*? No, but it does mean that you may have to employ another *strategy* to meet that objective. You could ask the librarian to get a copy on interloan for you. Or you could try another library. Or you could try to work out the particular chapters or pages you need and put in an interloan request for these to be copied for you.

5. Planning anything involves *breaking a process down into stages*, and learning to allocate time and resources to each stage. In studying, your most precious resource is often *time*, so work backwards from the final deadline:

- How long will you need to produce the final draft of your paper/essay, or to work through all the mock exam questions?
- How long will you need to revise your draft/s, to do your final exam revision?
- How long will you need to find and gather information, make notes, read, etc?

Obviously what you need to do changes with what you are aiming for, but the principle remains the same. Start by working backwards from the final deadline.

6. *Planning is specific.* Plan specifically:

- How many weeks/sessions will I need?
- Will I need help?
- Will I need equipment, access to computers, camera, etc?
- Where will I do it?
- When will I finish by?
- Have I allowed for contingencies and disasters? (They are inevitable!)

You should keep your master plan (see template at the end of this section) in your Learning Diary, and refer to it each night when you are making your brief entry in the diary. Scribble on it. Re-do it. But don't treat it as sacrosanct. Accept it as inevitable that, as you go along, the specifics will have to change, because circumstances always dictate this.

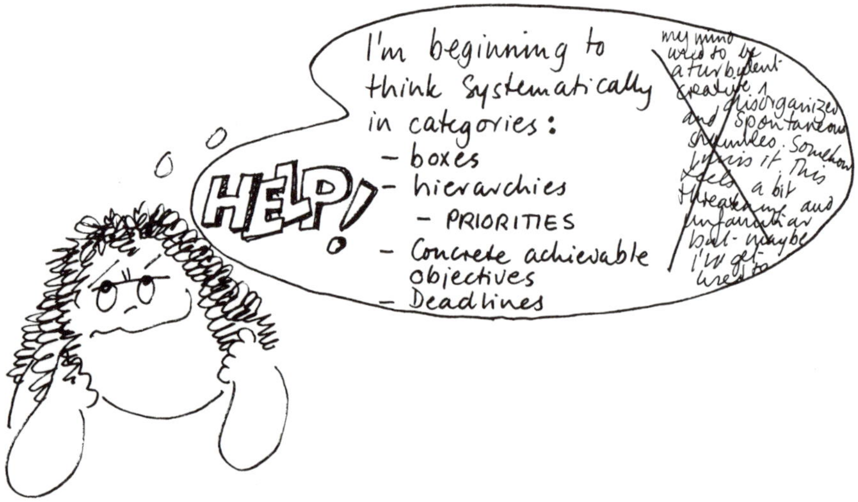

■ WHAT DO I WANT TO ACHIEVE?

Planning is not dreaming! When planning, you need to work out what you want to achieve and *state it in concrete and limited terms*. Your dream may well be to get a first-class degree, but you need concrete goals and objectives for each stage.

For example:

Aim:

To complete a year-long research project on the effects of TV on the pre-school child.

Goals:

1. To complete a literature review.
2. To interview a random sample of parents of pre-schoolers.
3. To complete five fieldwork studies using children in home settings.
4. To collate and compare the interview and fieldwork data with the findings of the literature survey.

Objectives:

Each of these goals would be further broken down into the exact process I would follow for, say, the literature review, and when I would achieve this objective.

It is this writing of concrete and achievable objectives that many people find difficult. There are many ways of writing objectives, but you may find this formula useful:

FORMULA	EXAMPLE
Given (conditions)	*Given* one and a half hours over the next five days
I will (achieve)	*I will* finish the book by Bogue on TV and toddlers
Doing (action taken)	*By reading* two chapters a day and making notes
When (by deadline)	*By* 20th July.

Example

Given two hours a day and access to the computer *I will* enter all my readings onto a database
By working from my cards in any order
By 4 December,i.e. 10 days.
The strategies that you use to achieve this objective, your day-to-day tactical plan, may include an even more detailed breakdown:
Day 1 : Design fields and use db software to compile
Day 2 : Enter 10 readings and try sorting
Day 3 - 10 : Enter remainder of readings.

■ HOW AM I GOING TO GET THERE?

Learning to break something down into *aims, goals, objectives* and *strategies* is the essence of planning technique, but the most significant constraint in planning is *you*, and your ability to use *personal planning strategies* as well as these planning techniques.

PERSONAL PLANNING

1. Work out when you function best. Are you a morning, afternoon or night person? Try to fit your most demanding work to your peak performance times.

2. Do you like to work in snatches throughout the day (assuming you have a day!) or do you work hard one day, none the next, or all morning, afternoon off, etc? Work out the *pattern* that gets most out of you and your available time.

3. Acknowledge that our concentration span is only 20-30 minutes, so, if you are planning an hour of study:

- Plan some 'warm-up' time — something to get you going and to focus your mind.
- Plan for 20-30 minutes of concentrated reading, study, writing.
- Plan a 'warm-down' — re-read, sort your notes, index them, list the main points, shut your eyes and concentrate on remembering the key concepts.

Preserve your mental stamina just as athletes preserve their physical stamina. This does not mean that you only plan to work for an hour at a time. You can plan to alternate intensive 'brain spurts' with mechanical tasks such as photocopying, sorting, filing.

Try to take a five-minute break every hour because your body, your lungs, your circulation need it.

4. It may be helpful to plan any task in chunks. If you don't finish, leave it there and *go on*. Keep to your allocated times. By the end of a week you will have got into your stride and you can go back and fill in the pieces.
Obviously this is not applicable to all learning tasks; in some cases you may find it useful for tasks like writing reports and essays where you say, for instance, 'Right, I'm going to finish the introduction by lunchtime'. You struggle, but you don't. Leave it, and come back to it later when you are refreshed.

5. You can allow for your own idiosyncrasies. Planning systematically does not mean that you have to work like an automaton from A to Z! It may be easier to start by writing the conclusion first and work backwards, leaving the introduction till last. If you suspect you are truly suffering from a block* (as opposed to the quite normal desire to procrastinate), start with something you like. In fact, start anywhere except at the beginning. Find a quote and write around it. Find a section you enjoyed at the time and begin your revision there. Accept that *how* you get there is your own choice. As long as you get there on time, does it matter whether you travelled by bus, helicopter or skateboard? Does it matter that you took a few dead ends and detours? The point of a plan is not its intrinsic beauty or worth, but whether it helps you to get to your destination. You need to plan, but don't make a bigger deal of the planning than your arrival at your destination!

* *When all else fails, vacuum the floor, mow the lawn or do the ironing! This is known as Displacement Therapy!*

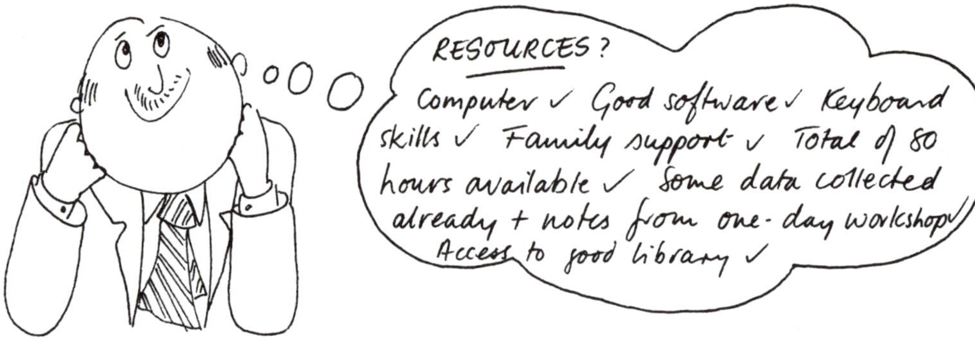

6. Identify constraints — what is stopping you from putting your plans into action — but do not dwell on them. Focus deliberately on your *resources* — what you have got to help you to your destination. *Time* is your most valuable resource, but resources also include your strengths and particular skills, like keyboard skills, family support, a friendly librarian, help with typing, an excellent and easily accessible library service.

SUMMARY

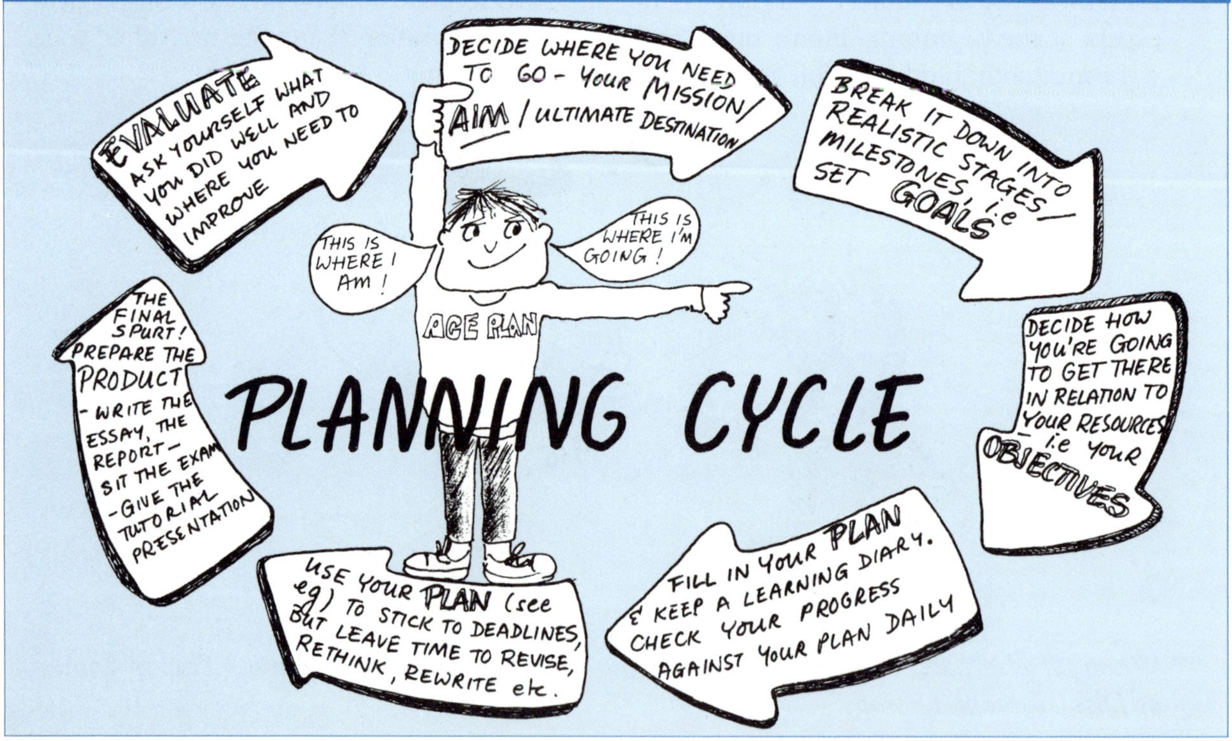

TIME PLANNING SHEET : TEMPLATE

TASK:		
DEADLINE:	TIME AVAILABLE:	
GOALS:	OBJECTIVES:	BY:
1	1.1	
	1.2	
	1.3	
	1.4	
	1.5	
2	2.1	
	2.2	
	2.3	
	2.4	
	2.5	
3	3.1	
	3.2	
	3.3	
	3.4	
	3.5	
4	4.1	
	4.2	
	4.3	
	4.4	
	4.5	
5	5.1	
	5.2	
	5.3	
	5.4	
	5.5	

OBJECTIVES
and strategies

TIME AVAILABLE: WEEKS

1	2	3	4	5	6	7	8	9	10	COMMENT

(see completed example overleaf)

TIME PLANNING SHEET : TEMPLATE

TASK: Research Project on effects of TV on preschool child

DEADLINE: 15/11/1990 TIME AVAILABLE: 7 months

GOALS:	OBJECTIVES:	BY:	
1 To complete a literature review	1.1 Manual search	10th April	Focus April/May
	1.2 Get online search	17th April	
	1.3 Interloans	no more after May	
	1.4 Establish database	3rd April	
	1.5 Read & enter on	30th May	
2 To interview a random sample of parents of preschoolers	2.1 Interview questionnaire design	start April, 30 May	Focus June
	2.2 trial	5th June	
	2.3 Revise	8th "	
	2.4 Interviews	25th "	
	2.5 Complete & collate	30th "	
3 To complete 5 fieldwork case studies using children in home settings	3.1 Establish research methodology	10 July	July/Aug
	3.2 Trial " "	15 "	
	3.3 Consult & adapt "	20 "	
	3.4 Set up case studies	31 "	
	3.5 Case studies: supervise	→ 30 Aug	
4 To collate and compare the interview & fieldwork data with the findings of the literature survey	4.1		September
	4.2		
	4.3		
	4.4		
	4.5		
5 To prepare drafts and final copy	5.1		October
	5.2		
	5.3		
	5.4		
	5.5		

OBJECTIVES and strategies

TIME AVAILABLE: WEEKS 8

	1	2	3	4	5	6	7	8	~~9~~	~~10~~	COMMENT
Goal 1	April				May						
1.1 manual search	→	→									
1.2 online "	→	→	→								
1.3 interloans	Ongoing for the whole 2 months →										try not to get any more interloan stuff after end may.
1.4 database 1.5 Read & enter data	Set-up → Enter data on ongoing basis →										Ongoing for whole project — leave time on next chart

Thinking Skills

- WHAT THINKING STRATEGIES DO I NEED FOR EFFECTIVE LEARNING?
- HOW DO I REMEMBER MORE AND FORGET LESS?

OVERVIEW

Thinking skills and kinds of learning are closely aligned. Just as everybody uses every kind of learning, but finds one or two kinds more comfortable, so everybody is capable of the whole range of analytic and creative thinking strategies. The benefit, once again, comes from making systematic and conscious use of as many strategies as possible — expanding your repertoire.

Ten of these strategies are explored in this section. These strategies are used in the reading and research sections (7-10), and are useful for exam revision and for self-evaluation (sections 11 and 12).

How you learn is, to a large extent, determined by how you learn to think.

Analytic thinking skills include the ability to think:

- *linearly and logically,* in a step-by-step way,
- *hypothetically and scientifically,* establishing a 'what if?' hypothesis, collecting and examining clues and data to confirm or reject it,
- *deductively,* piecing together the evidence and drawing conclusions.

Creative thinking skills include the ability to think:

- *laterally* and *imaginatively,* looking at all sides of an issue, turning something around and looking at it in a totally different way, devising interesting and imaginative solutions, pursuing unexpected and different lines of thought,
- *intuitively,* being able to 'feel' your way using trained instinct, thinking your way through a situation by imagining yourself in someone else's shoes or head.

The 10 strategies introduced in this section include the three core skills, the gears, which drive the learning process.

In Section 1 we looked at seven types of learning — rote, narrative, visual, verbal, analytic, multi-sense/emotional and symbolic/numeric. We also considered four approaches to learning — builders, bakers, boffins, butlers. Here we suggest that there are *two main types of thinking,* and *two main types of thinkers,* and that there is a relationship between the type of learner you are and the type of thinker you are.

- If you enjoy clear step-by-step explanations, insist on logical reasons before you accept an explanation, like things to be clear-cut, to the point, factual rather than subjective and emotional, you are predominantly a *linear* or *convergent* thinker. Convergent thinkers are often builders, boffins and sometimes butlers when it comes to learning. It is rare to find a baker who is equally at home in linear/ convergent and creative/ divergent thinking modes.
- If you enjoy thinking through possibilities, conquering new theory, using ingenuity to solve problems, you are probably a *creative* or *divergent* thinker. You are likely to see problems as challenges rather than crises, and you may find that you get impatient with people who don't share your pleasure in looking at the future and get bogged down in the nitty-gritty of prosaic everyday detail.

  You are inevitably a baker in your approach to learning. It is surprising how many butlers are closet bakers! By this I mean that many have tremendous potential for creative, divergent thinking, but have always held back with a wait-and-see approach.

We all use all types of learning and thinking, but most of us have a preference, a predominant type. This can have a profound effect on how we approach learning and teaching, as is illustrated in the story on p. 47. But before you read it, try the task yourself.

There is a steep piece of ground covered with trees. You are going to build a house. Spend five minutes jotting down what you would do first.

1. First I would
2. Then I would
3. Next I would

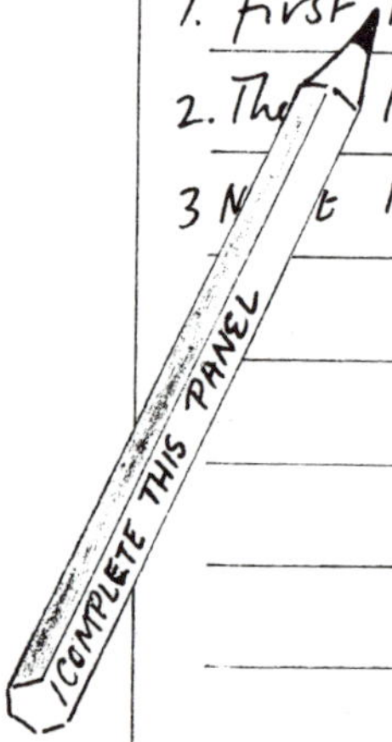

Example

A group of people was told that they had a steep piece of ground covered with trees, and they were going to build a house. First they had to spend five minutes jotting down what they would do. At the end of the five minutes they shared what they had written.

It became clear that people had seen two quite distinct ways of approaching the task.

Irrespective of age, sex, race or occupation, some people began by asking practical and very necessary questions about building regulations, sewerage, gradients, access for bulldozers, etc.

Others began immediately to design the house, describing in some detail how it would soar over the trees, hug the contour of the hill, integrate with the landscape, etc. Once they knew what they wanted, they'd sort out the details!

Both groups could see that neither way was intrinsically 'better', although each remained convinced that theirs was the 'right' way! Both groups were staggered that, given the same task and the same instructions, it was possible to interpret it in vastly different ways.

People who are strongly linear/convergent prefer to build up from a level of solving details one by one. Strongly creative/divergent thinkers tend to do the opposite, trying to grasp the whole concept, see the whole issue before they break it down into steps.

The way we think is the way we perceive reality. If there is a large gap between the way one person perceives something and the way another person perceives it, it is known as *cognitive dissonance,* and it can be a barrier to good communication.

Think of a strongly *linear* teacher explaining something to a strongly *creative/divergent* student. If you were explaining to me step-by-step how to build a house, I'd think you were a boring old pedant, because what I want to know is what type of house, what design, will it be exciting hill-hugging wood, or dramatic, intrusive concrete and stainless steel? The obvious answer is to try to become flexible in using both convergent and divergent approaches.

We *all* use both all the time anyway. It's just a matter of becoming more conscious about using your non-predominant mode.

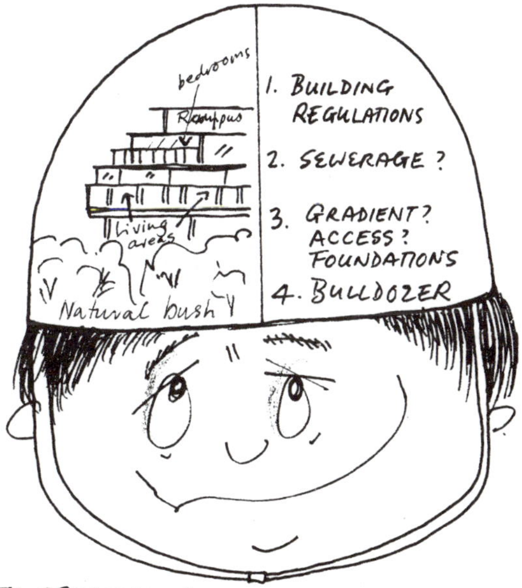

WITH CREATIVE AND LINEAR THINKING SKILLS UNDER MY HARD HAT, I SHOULD END UP WITH A WELL THOUGHT OUT HOUSE!

This story shows all the key thinking skills in action:

Once there was a farmer who needed more room for grazing, so he decided to chop down a small wood. First he went out to **survey and map** the wood because he wanted to get an overview. How many trees were there? What kinds? Were any valuable for timber? Were there any native trees? Could he cut them down himself? How long would it take?

Then he sat down and **grouped and categorised** : types of trees/ valuable trees/ firewood trees/ small trees which he could cut down himself/ big trees where he would need help. By the time he had finished, he had a clear idea of the size of the task.

Then he **compared** how long it would take if he did it himself with the cost of employing labour and saving his time, and he listed **the pros and cons**. By the time he was starting to enjoy himself, he listed all the key factors in his decisions — cost/time/profit/other urgent farm work/possible tax considerations/ecological considerations.

By this stage he thought it was worthwhile to write down all the **questions** that were buzzing around in his head.

Who should do it — himself or employed labour?

What needed to be done — cut down trees, or cut into pieces for transport?

Where could he store the wood or sell the firewood?

How — chainsaw, brute force and tractor, or would he have to hire a bulldozer?

Why — is the cost/effort/reward worth it for the extra grazing? Does the loss of the wood devalue the property? What would provide shade for the cows in the heat of summer? How much will the extra grazing earn in hard dollar terms?

Finally, his head buzzing, he began to think it through as a **problem**. If, he **hypothesised**, he spent the money clearing the wood, would the cost of hiring help be offset by any profit from selling the timber and firewood? And would the long-term financial benefits of the extra grazing compensate for the loss of some beautiful trees, and shade for the animals?

He **analysed** all the information he had gleaned by putting his list of questions to officials and farming colleagues. It didn't really add up. Cutting down the wood was a solution, sure, but maybe not the best one for this particular problem when he **interpreted** all the available data. In fact, his wife was always **inferring** that he was saw-happy, cutting down anything that moved without thinking it through.

Meanwhile something in the tax advice was niggling at the back of his mind, so he decided to think **laterally,** turn the thing on its head and look at it another way. If what he wanted was more grazing, why not hire it when he needed it and qualify for tax exemption? His wife would approve, the cows would approve and they would keep their beautiful trees.

■ WHAT THINKING STRATEGIES DO I NEED FOR EFFECTIVE LEARNING?

BRAINSTORMING

1. Whether you do it alone or in a group, it is a good technique for working out what you know already, freeing your thinking up, letting your mind slide over ideas, associations, related and unrelated issues, suspending judgement, triggering lateral thinking ...

How to do it:

Working alone: Take paper, set a timer and give yourself approximately five minutes. Write down the topic/ issue/ subject you are brainstorming. Then *write* down, as fast as you can, *anything* that comes to mind — facts, figures, dates, associations, related issues. Don't stop, don't worry about the value, relevance or correctness of what you are jotting down. Just write until you cannot think of another thing, or until the buzzer goes.

In a group: As above, but ideas are called out, and a totally impartial, objective, non-judging scribe writes it all down on a board/ chart, and *no one* is allowed to comment on or pass judgement on anyone's suggestions. The process is a totally non-critical, non-judgemental one.

Example of Three-Minute Brainstorm

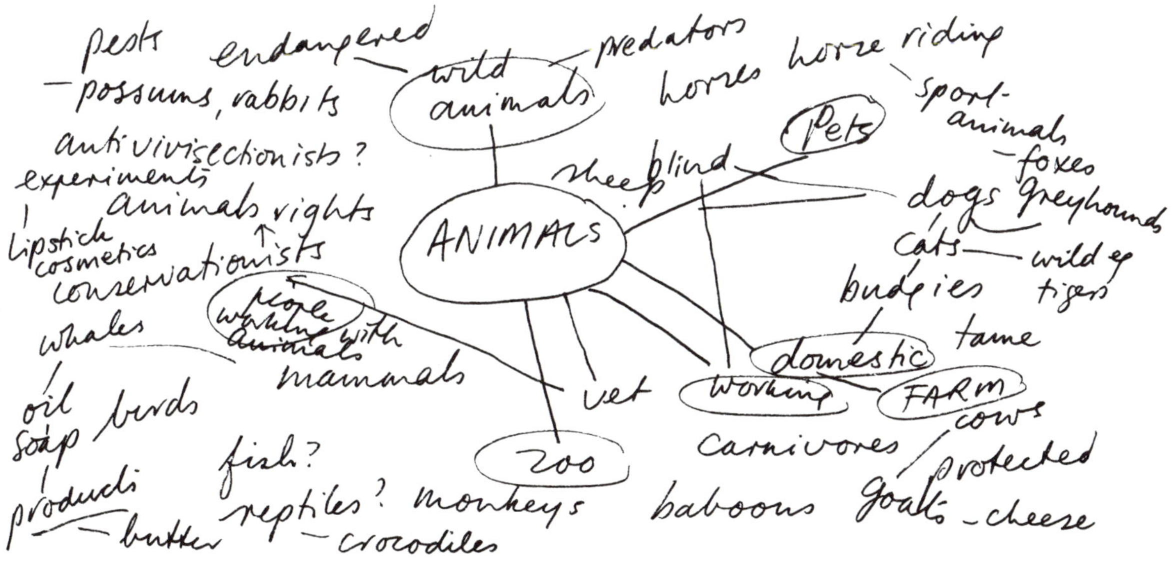

MAPPING

2. This means drawing the extent and scope, an overview, of the topic. You can do it as a *spidergram* (as in example 1) or a *lineargram* (see example 2), or as a *timeline* (see example 3), or any way that suits you and the topic.

Mapping is often a technique that goes hand in hand with brainstorming. Using the next strategy, categorising and ordering, you group and label the elements in your brainstorming chart into similar categories or clusters, and make them into a mental map.

Mapping is often called webbing, semantic networking, or cognitive mapping. Either way, *mapping is the single most valuable thinking and learning strategy*, the one you cannot afford to do without.

Your map provides you with the signposts you need for planning your task, reading and researching, organising and filing your notes, planning and writing essays, reports, theses, and for revising and structuring your study.

EXAMPLES OF MAPPING

Example 1

Spidergram Mapping

The main topic is the body of the spider. Sub-topics are the legs of the spider. Aspects of these sub-topics are hairs on the legs of the spider, and so on ...

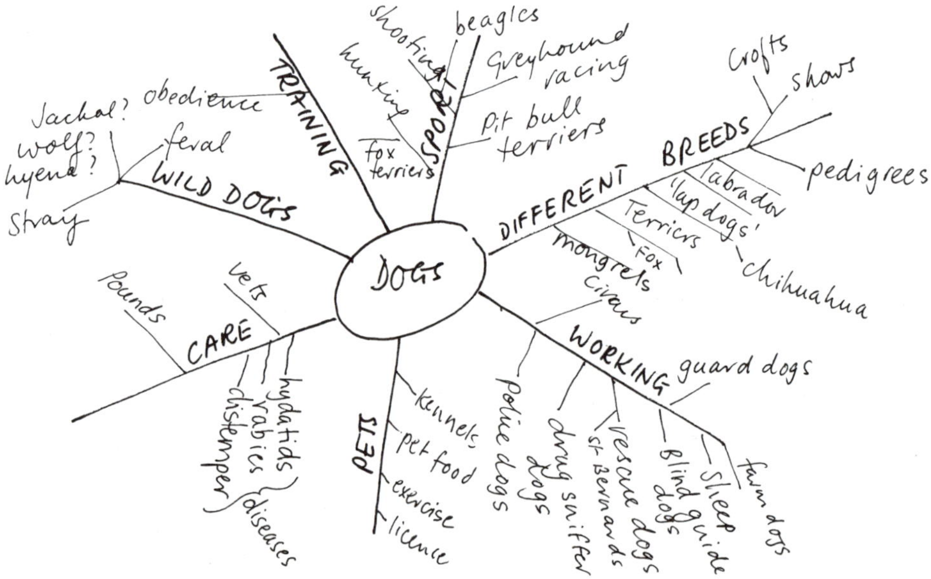

Example 2

Linear Mapping

The main topic is, likewise, broken down into sub-topics and aspects of these sub-topics, working downwards from simple to complex, from broad-brush to detailed.

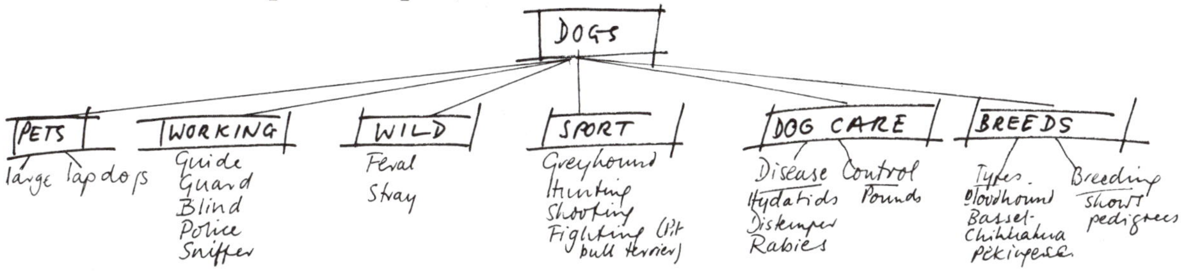

Example 3

Timeline

A historical topic can be mapped as a timeline, using 100-year periods, decades or significant dates as signposts. (Adapted from the *Macmillan Encyclopaedia of Art*, 1977.)

APPROX. 2500 BC – Neolithic settlements in Crete
> 2500 – 2000 BC – Early Minoan period – first important Aegean civilization
1750 BC – Palace at Knossos – bullfighting, dancing, writing
1700 BC – First palace destroyed by earthquake
1550 BC – Shaft graves at Mycenae
1500 BC – Knossos destroyed
1400 BC – Mycenean culture replacing Minoan
Acheans invade Greece

CATEGORISING AND ORDERING

3. Grouping items, ideas, concepts into categories that are similar, deciding what is most and least important within each category, and being able to rank the items from general to specific and vice versa.

If you can't see the wood for the trees, you start by deciding what is not a tree, then looking for similar types of trees, then ranking them by height maturity or value. This seems obvious, but any examiner will attest that one of the main reasons people fail is not that they did not know the material, but that they could not sort it into any meaningful order. They did not seem to be able to distinguish between what was important and what was marginal.

This is a simple strategy, but a key one. It is easier to apply to finite objects, like dogs or trees, but much more challenging when it comes to concepts and global or basket topics like ecology, pollution, childcare or politics. Try it!

COMPARING AND CONTRASTING

4. This is something we all do all the time, but there are several useful techniques :

a) An interesting technique derived from a psychology / management technique known as Repertory Grid Analysis involves taking three items and asking what two of them have in common that makes them different from the third.

Example

compare :
① CAT
② HORSE
③ AIRCRAFT

②+③ "ridden" by humans
①+② have 4 legs // wings – animals // machine
②+③ means of transport – used in battle
①+② organic waste – don't contribute to pollution
①+③ both climb // horses don't [what about Shetland ponies?]
①+② can't rust – self propelled // needs fuel – eat food
②+③ used for sport

This may seem a spurious example, but it is an excellent activity for mental limbering up and triggering lateral thinking juices because it releases all sorts of possibilities which would not have occurred to you otherwise.

b) Similarities and differences can also stretch the mind. Try this one:

Similarities and differences

S = similar
D = different

	JOAN OF ARC		MAHATMA GANDHI
1	woman	D	man
2	Born 1412	D	Born 1869
3	1920 declared saint	S	Mahatma = "Great soul"
4	Denounced as a witch	S	imprisoned several times

c) Pros and cons : listing the fors and againsts of any situation, person or issue can force you to think logically, overcome your own biases and fixed thought patterns.

Example

CHOPPING DOWN THE WOOD

FOR	AGAINST
1. Need more grazing	1. Need to hire bulldozer
2. Need $ from timber	2. " " employ labour
3. Could sell rest as firewood	3. Will take time
4. Will give us supply of "	4. Pity to lose native trees
5. Could do a lot of the work myself – cheap	5. Will lose shade for cows
	6. $ from timber may not pay for bulldozer + labour?
	7. Wife anti – loss of beauty spot
	8. No tax advantage

KEY WORDS AND CONCEPTS

5. This, like mapping, is a key cognitive strategy, and they work closely together.

You need key *words* and *terms* for all aspects of your learning:

- to describe what you know already
- to structure your reading and research
- to look up in catalogues, indexes, contents pages
- to keep in your mind's eye when you scan for information
- to use as a peg for your interview questions if your information source is a person.

Your *map* provides your first set of key terms and words (see. p. 50) — working/dogs wild dogs/ pets dogs/ dog breeding/ breeding dogs/ disease control, etc. Your map also provides the general to specific structure which is helpful for looking things up. For example, if you were looking in a card catalogue, you might be better advised to look up 'cats' before you try 'Siamese cats'.

Another method of listing the key words, terms and concepts you need to build your cognitive structure of the subject is looking for an overview (in a general encyclopaedia, book or pamphlet) and listing the key words to fix them in your head.

Example* **INFORMATION?**

point in learning techniques for using information until you have given some thought to what exactly information is. Is information facts, data, knowledge, or wisdom? Is it facts lying in an encyclopaedia waiting to be photocopied?

This book is based on a view of information as **process**, not a product or commodity.

Information is the process of becoming informed

It is the process of adding to the store of your experience more or less consciously by using the experience of others — real, or filtered through their imaginations, and stored in print, film, maps, pictures, video discs, fiction, 'non-fiction', biography, and in people sources. **Information informs us.** It is not 'facts'.

WHAT ARE INFORMATION SKILLS?

Information skills are the skills needed to make efficient and effective use of information. Traditionally we have seen and taught this complex of skills in a fragmented way — as reading skills, comprehension skills, library skills, study skills, notemaking skills. To use information effectively you need reading listening, viewing, observing, 'library', and retrieval skills; you need to know how to skim, scan, select, reject, analyse, and synthesise, and present information selectively, with originality and impact.

* Gawith, Gwen *Information Alive!*, Auckland: Longman Paul, 1987.

KEY WORDS KEY TERMS, KEY CONCEPTS

facts / data / knowledge / wisdom } info.

information process

print / film / maps / video / pictures / videodiscs / fiction / non-fiction } formats

skills • reading • comprehension • listening • viewing • library • study • retrieval

Process skim > scan > select > reject > analyse interpret > present

ASKING QUESTIONS

6. Questions — or the ability to shape them — are often the missing link in effective research, reading, revision and study. They help to pin down what you need to know, what is important. They form the basic structure from which you analyse your information, and they give structure to what you write and say. Simply, if it begins with a W or an H, it is a question :

WHO
WHAT
WHY
WHERE
WHEN
HOW

?

Who, what, where, when and *how* are the basis of fact-finding, of gathering the information. *Why* is the question you ask to analyse, infer, interpret, deduce, draw conclusions, inferences and implications. In other words, it is better to accumulate as much impartial and objective information as possible before you apply the powerful 'why?' for the analysis and interpretation of this information.

FORMULATING PROBLEMS AND HYPOTHESES

7. The ability to see a situation as a problem, or as a 'what if?' hypothesis. Working through possible causes, effects, solutions or reasons is an important skill in your thinking armoury.

Example 1

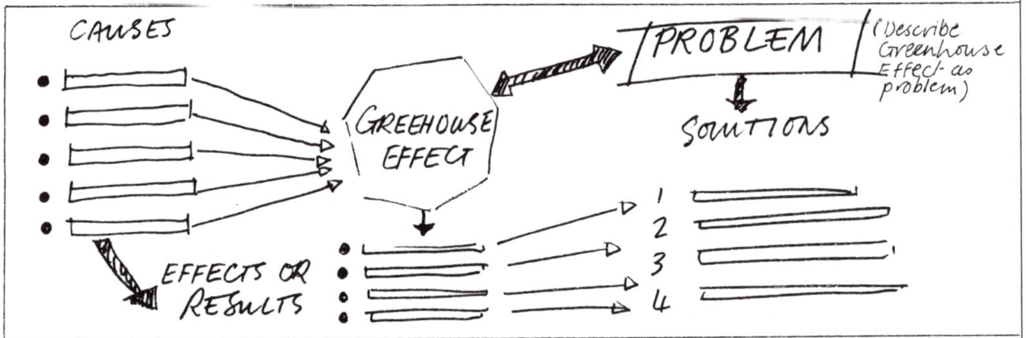

Example 2

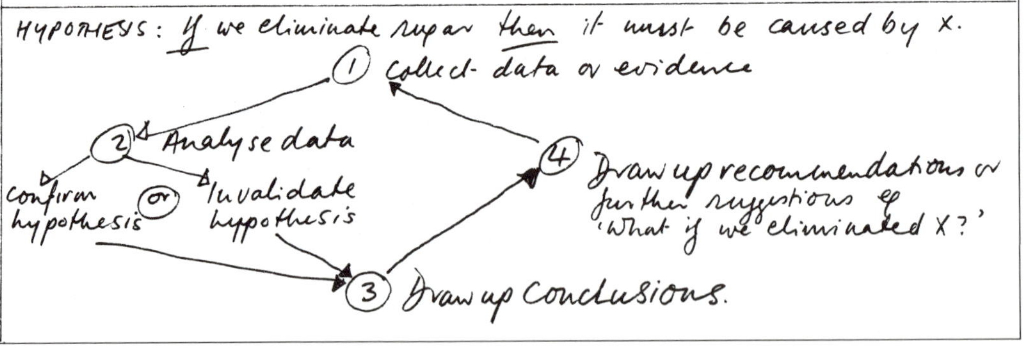

ANALYSING, INFERRING, INTERPRETING

8. Looking critically and objectively to discriminate, describe, predict, challenge, suggest, argue, draw conclusions, prove, examine all aspects and angles. Some would argue that this is the essence of thinking — that these are the capacities that distinguish humans from animals. True, and all the more reason to focus on them and hone them into precision cognitive tools!

Analysing means setting out deliberately to look at the parts — the causes, the reasons, facts, figures, data, opinions and applying the processes we have already discussed, i.e. *categorising and ordering* (3), *comparing and contrasting* (4), asking *questions* (6), and *formulating problems and hypotheses* (7).

Inferring means reading between the lines, reading for meanings that are not directly stated, spelling out what is implied.

Interpreting means putting your own ideas on show, saying what *you* think it means.

<u>Example</u>

The farmer and his tree dilemma made good use of analytical thinking skills.

He didn't just say a tree is a tree is a tree! He **categorised and ordered** the trees into valuable/not valuable, I can cut down/I can't, native/non-native.

He **compared and contrasted** the pros and cons using different elements — cost in time, cost in money, cost in loss of shade/beauty.

This analysis showed him that he needed to reformulate the **questions**. Originally he'd asked, 'How can I get more grazing?' Now the question became, 'What will I gain and lose by chopping down the trees? Will the acquisition of more grazing compensate for the permanent loss of valuable trees, shade and beauty?'

In turn he began to see the **problem** differently. Maybe the problem wasn't that he had too little grazing, but that he had too many cattle? So, instead of thinking through the answers to the question just in terms of 'What will I gain or lose by chopping down the trees?' he also thought it through in terms of 'What do I gain or lose by having so many cattle?'

He formulated a new hypothesis: 'If I regard my trees as permanent but my cattle numbers as flexible, then I can adjust my cattle numbers and the amount of extra grazing I have to hire to market prices for meat.' This would have led him to consider the possibility that his hypothesis might be flawed. Maybe the cost of hiring extra grazing was also tied into market demand? He'd have to investigate this first.

What he **inferred** from all this was that value was relative. His wife might have been right about his saw-happy behaviour in the past. Not that he'd admit it, of course! But, given the fact that he now had all the information, and could **interpret** it in the light of a really thorough assessment of cost, value, short- and long-term benefits, he felt that whatever he decided it would be a better decision because he'd thought it through, not just in his head, but on paper.

This blow-by-blow look at what was happening in the farmer's head illustrates that cognitive skills are not sequential. You don't analyse, compare and contrast and then cross it off the list and start formulating questions. All the skills and processes are mixed, and you keep on going back to the first step of breaking it down and thinking it through in the light of yet another question or problem.

There is absolutely nothing new here. We all debate issues in our heads all the time. The difference is the degree of consciousness. The farmer actually sat down with pen and paper and worked through it systematically.

This leads to very different results from just running it through in your own head. You simply are not objective enough, whereas a dialogue with yourself on paper introduces the element of objectivity you need for thorough analysis.

This has been explored in some depth because it also illustrates the two skills that follow, deducing and lateral thinking. What the farmer did was to apply different questions to the information he had gathered (feelings as well as facts and figures).

Treating the information as clues, he was able to deduce different solutions. He could see now how limited he'd been in his original approach, asking, 'How can I get more grazing?' and only seeing one answer, 'Chop down the trees!' He became a born again thinker!

DEDUCING

9. 'Deducing' is, in fact, the same as inferring. The dictionary definition of 'deduce' is 'Infer by reasoning from given facts'. But because students at all levels find it difficult, it has been treated as a separate strategy.

It is easier to describe what you think, feel, believe, to give your views and opinions, than to *suppress* what you think and feel, and employ *reasoning* skills to let the information speak for itself.

Working with school students, I am often struck by the strong feelings and opinions they claim and how little data, evidence and hard facts they can dredge up to support their stance. They often ignore even the little evidence that is staring them in the face if it contradicts a cherished opinion.

There is no quick recipe. Deducing requires the learner to read like a detective, collect all the evidence, and analyse it with a rigour and objectivity driven by the catch phrase, 'Let the information speak for itself'.

THINKING LATERALLY

10. The skill of making mental links which Edward de Bono popularised as a cognitive art form is triggered by many of the processes described here, but the best trigger I have met was given to me years ago by a tutor who continuously asked, 'But what if the opposite were true?'

Other techniques, like imagining yourself inside another's shoes or head, seeing the situation, speaking the words as that person would, limber your mind up for the effortless leaps and links that characterise the lateral thinker.

Associations are at the heart of lateral thinking, and forcing yourself to brainstorm *with a pencil* can unlock associations you didn't know your mind was capable of making. Brainstorming is the fuel of lateral thinking, and comparing and contrasting techniques (4) are part of the training apparatus. Seeing how the farmer pushes his thinking a bit further illustrates this.

Example

By this stage the farmer was so delighted with being a born again thinker that he couldn't help himself.

He looked again at all the information he'd assembled. What kept on niggling at him was why his wife had been so furious with him. She normally didn't interfere with his farming decisions, but in this case she was really angry. He couldn't work out why. She'd kept on saying that it was the most beautiful spot on the farm, and didn't he have any soul? Well, the cows liked it, but he didn't fancy their chances in the soul stakes. Anyway, he'd go and look at it again. When he got there, he had to admit that his wife had a point. It really was lovely, and you could see for ever. In fact, if you turned around and shut and opened your eyes you could see a dozen different pictures.

This triggered something in his mind. Maybe beauty had a market value. Maybe it was a question of finding the market. He suggested to his wife that possibly they could advertise in town and charge a small entry fee for painting clubs and classes. She saw the potential immediately and suggested that if she could offer a large and luscious cream tea, they could charge a reasonable fee and she'd be happy to run it as her part of the business. Needless to say, they lived happily ever after, he farming and she running Farm Paint and Tea Trips!

The point of this story is that *lateral* thinking seldom happens suddenly. It is usually the result of a lot of conscious and unconscious thinking — thinking through every angle of a problem, turning it around and examining it from the other side, as the farmer did.

There is no doubt that strongly creative/divergent thinkers find it easier to make these mental lateral leaps than strongly convergent/linear thinkers. The farmer's story shows that they are not mutually exclusive.

Anyone who thinks through a situation systematically, whether their natural preference is for linear or creative thinking, has a better chance of coming up with interesting and inventive solutions than someone who sits around convinced that somehow inspiration will strike!

Thinking is *work*, whether your natural propensity is for creative or linear processes. Force your hand to be an extension of your mind by drawing out your ideas, making lists or brainstorming.

The three key skills or gears introduced here will underpin each of the sections to follow. They are:

- **Mapping** (shorthand for brainstorming, sorting, categorising)
- **Key wording** (shorthand for working out the key terms and concepts)
- **Questions** (shorthand for formulating questions, problems, 'what ifs').

Later sections will show how each of these skills is adapted to a wide variety of learning situations.

HOW DO I REMEMBER MORE?

To improve how much you can remember, and for how long, there are some techniques you can practise. These relate to, and they should be read in conjunction with, many of the cognitive strategies already described.

MIND MAPS

1. (see p. 50) These are a good technique, not just for breaking down a topic into its constituent parts, but as a peg for your memory. You can teach yourself to draw mind maps in your head when you listen to a talk, read a book, or even when you are introduced to several people and you want to remember their names. Mind maps can be used with visual and verbal associations (see below) as a powerful focus for your memory.

ASSOCIATIONS

2. You can use visual or verbal associations consciously to trigger your memory. We all use associations; a piece of music reminds us of a person. You can do it deliberately by 'labelling' an incident, person or idea.

You are introduced to a number of people. You 'map' them in your mind's eye (see *mind maps* above) and then you work out associations. Jean and Jo are married. They become the J's. Your stepmother is Eileen, so you'll remember Eileen. Helen and Miles could be married so you think of them as Hm? and, finally, Harry Mills is tall and bearded, so he'll always be Hairy Windmill!

Tony Buzan has written a number of books on thinking and memory. He recommends remembering numbers by associating them with rhyming words. I find this impossible; for me it's easier to remember numbers by visualising them in bright letters on a TV screen in my head, or written up in glowing neon! Visual learners find it easier to remember anything if they *write it down.*

VISUALISING

3. As with the number example above, consciously setting out to see things in your head — on the TV screen in your head, if you like — may help. Train yourself to visualise pictures, diagrams, scenes, physical movements (like seeing yourself play golf, or doing a dance step). Training yourself to recall the image on demand is a useful skill. It is possible to learn history by seeing it as a video in your head. You can remember the protagonists of a novel by seeing them in your head as a group photograph.

CATEGORISING, GROUPING, ORDERING

4. (see p. 51) It makes sense to reduce a number of discrete items to several groups. This is the principle behind many of the memory training games and tests in 'train your memory' books. By remembering items by associating them with categories, such as fruit, weather or sports, you have a better chance of remembering them than as individual items such as clouds, hockey, tennis, rain, apples, tornadoes, melons.

The more you can group, order and sort, the better your mental filing system will be for recall, just as a good indexing system is the secret of any filing or records management system, or catalogue.

Categories with easily memorised or unique labels or keywords/terms (see p. 53) are most effective.

DIAGRAMS

5. This is really a combination and extension of mapping, visualising and categorising. It involves translating information into an easily remembered graphic or diagram.

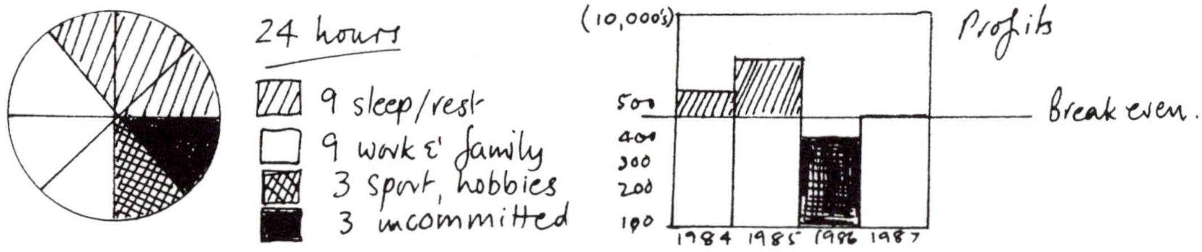

Pie charts and graphs are useful for remembering quantities.

Ladders are useful for procedures.
So are steps, timelines, flow diagrams, pyramids and ideographs.

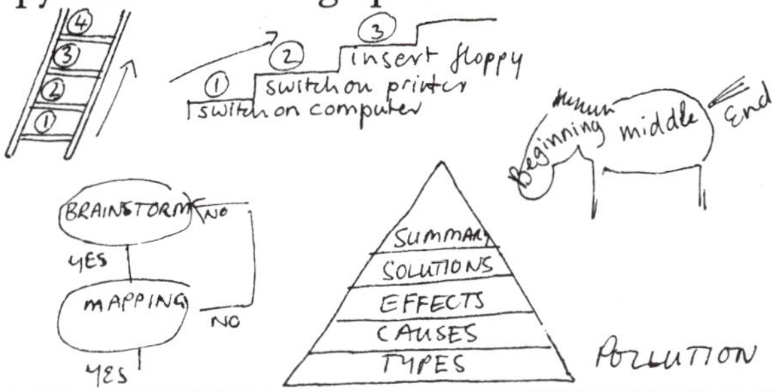

Draw them on paper, or on the TV screen in your mind, but shut your eyes and 'see' it. Repeat this until you can recall the diagram with no difficulty. All you will ever need, then, is a brief look to retrigger it.

Words are the most difficult things to memorise, so reduce the word-burden on your memory by condensing as much as you can into diagrams and pictures. This is particularly important with exam revision.

VERBALISING

6. The act of giving words to thoughts helps to commit them to memory. Like all memories, words we remember from childhood can recede if they are not used for years. But, like any long-term memory, you need only a brief exposure to re-activate and recharge that memory.

Saying things aloud, writing them down, using any technique you can think of to fix the words in your memory all help.

The well-known study formula SQ3R makes heavy use of verbalising and other techniques we have discussed, like formulating your own questions and speaking the answers in your own words in your head. So you *s*tudy a text, you recall the important bits as *q*ueries or *q*uestions, and then you *r*ead, *r*ecite and *r*eview it, anchoring it in your memory with *words.*

Key words are an important verbal memory trigger, and can be impressed even more firmly onto your mind if you can *see* and *hear* the key word in your mind simultaneously.

COMBINATIONS

7. Using your fingers may help here. When I am giving a talk, a tutorial presentation or going to an interview, I try to rehearse no more than five main points. Then I can count them off on my fingers! Or, if I know I have five main ideas, then I try to visualise them as five boxes, and systematically unpack the contents.

You can see the same thing as a linear diagram, but this may be more useful when you are writing. Seeing boxes, baskets or something tangible that you can literally unpack in your mind may be more helpful for verbal presentations of any kind.

Ultimately each person develops individual techniques which may not work for anyone else.

You need to become conscious of how *your* memory appears to fire itself. Work on the techniques you are already good at, trying to improve them, and also try to expand your repertoire by experimenting with a few new techniques. Remember that anything new will feel awkward in the beginning, so persevere!

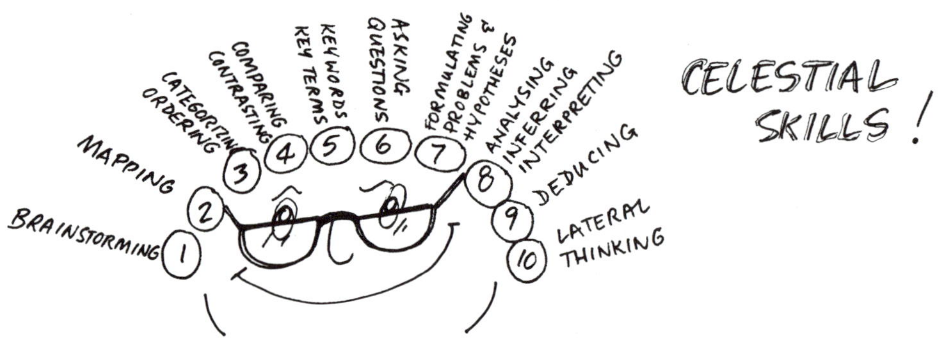

SUMMARY

Cognitive or thinking skills are the skills you need to:

1. Work out what you know already by **brainstorming**.
2. See the scope, the overview, by **mapping or diagramming** it.
3. Structure it by **sorting, categorizing, grouping**.
4. Label these **key concepts, words and terms** for retrieval, recall.
5. Develop the topic as a series of **questions**.
6. Describe it as a **problem or hypothesis**.
7. **Compile, collate and compare** the data.
8. **Analyse, make inferences and interpretations** from the data.
9. **Deduce**, draw conclusions, devise solutions, make recommendations.
10. **Think laterally**, see links, opposites or the unrelated.

Many thinking skills and strategies are also useful tools for improving your memory. How you remember is linked to what type of thinker and learner you are. You need to be conscious of your strengths and competencies and build on them, but also work quite consciously to use these thinking/memory strategies to expand your repertoire.

Study Skills and Habits

■ IS THERE A RECIPE FOR INSTANT SUCCESS?

OVERVIEW

Most books on study skills are not really about skills, but about study *habits*. And rightly so. Any habit is a skill that is practised until it becomes automatic. Any skill can atrophy if it is not practised.

Many of the skills introduced in Sections 1-6, like mapping, categorising, visualising and framing questions, can become instinctive habits, *if* you practise them consciously and continuously. The glue that holds them together, the most valuable study habit of all, is the habit of *planning* as outlined in Section 4.

The essence of effective study is the use of *planning, time management* and *self-appraisal* techniques on a *regular* basis so that study and research skills and strategies become internalised and habitual. Without planning, time management and evaluation, developing study skills into study habits is the luck of the draw, unpredictable and random.

This section revises some of the key elements of planning. It looks at *regular revision* as the most useful, and most neglected, of study habits. It introduces a formula to make study and revision more effective.

At the heart of effective study habits is the idea that the skills and strategies introduced in this book are used *every day*. There is a tendency for people to regard study skills as something they keep in mothballs until the big event of revision and exams; when you really need them is *throughout* the year.

By the end of the year, you should be on automatic pilot in terms of study skills and habits. You can't expect to leave it to the end of the year to shovel in huge lumps of content *and* learn skills and habits at the same time!

■ IS THERE A RECIPE FOR INSTANT SUCCESS?

Simply *no!* Some have claimed that putting notes under your pillow or running a tape in the dead hours of the night works. The only answer is to try it and see what you think! There are two keywords in effective study habits:

PLANNING

This complements what was discussed in Section 4 on personal planning.

Books on study skills often talk about a quiet room, concentration span, rewarding your own efforts and developing memory techniques. While all these are valuable, if you're going to develop study habits that suit *you,* your constraints (time, family, other occupations) and your natural inclinations (when you work best, the type of learner you are), you need to try out different patterns and plan to get the most out of yourself in a way that suits you best.

You may find that you can concentrate for longer stretches in the morning. You may do what I do when I can afford the time: I beat my brains out in a 12-14 hour marathon, and then take the next day off to skate, flop around and vacuum. Other people find it better to pace themselves steadily.

There is no virtue in any one pattern, but it needs to work *for you* so:

- Work out the optimum conditions for you.
- Plan to work regularly using this pattern, remembering the point that study skills and strategies only become study habits if they are practised regularly.
- Use your Learning Diary to set weekly targets. Fill in your Learning Diary daily, use your time planner hourly (see p. 33).

Get used to talking to yourself — having an internal dialogue! It is another key study habit. If it feels easier, think of it as a conversation with your Learning Diary. Think of your diary asking you 'Ok, so what did you learn today?' 'Could you reconstruct it from the notes you made? 'Did you achieve all the objectives you wrote down?' If you are tough with yourself, teachers, lecturers, examiners will seem soft by comparison! (More strategies for self-appraisal will be given in Section 12.)

REGULAR REVISION

Revision means re-studying material which has already been studied. If this seems self-evident, consider the proposition that, for many people, revision is not *re*-studying something studied before, but studying it properly *for the first time.*

If you attend lectures, file your lecture notes and then study them just before an exam, that is *not* revision. Yet for most of us this is what passes for revision, and we blame *exams* for being stressful. It does not matter how fair the questions are, the stress comes from forcing yourself to digest huge slabs of totally unprocessed cognitive fodder!

What is suggested here is like comparing the difference between adding hot water to instant coffee, and growing the coffee beans, harvesting and roasting them, grinding them and percolating the brew, all in the time it takes to boil the kettle!

There are several concepts about revision which you need to internalise:

- Revision is regular, continuous.
- Revision is the cornerstone of learning.
- Revision is an ongoing process — before-exam revision is the end of the process.

Revision can be shaped into a formula-driven set of steps and procedures which are integrated to your long-term and daily planning and become a relatively painless habit, part of your whole approach to learning, not an end-of-the-year bogey.

RULE 1

Revision is done *daily*. The important thing is to be able to think about and *note* the important points in whatever you have done — lectures, reading, seminars, workshops — as soon afterwards as possible. If you can't do this the same day, what are your chances of recalling the information at the end of the year?

RULE 2

At the *end of the week* you revise the whole week's work. This need not be laborious if you have done your 10-minute revision every day. This weekly revision need take no more than 15-20 minutes.

RULE 3

At the end of the month when you are looking back at your time planning sheets, your Learning Diary and your planning, spend at least an hour revising everything done to date. This does not mean a massive orgy of re-reading and masochism, but merely going through your revision prompts — your maps, notes, diagrams (see p. 50).

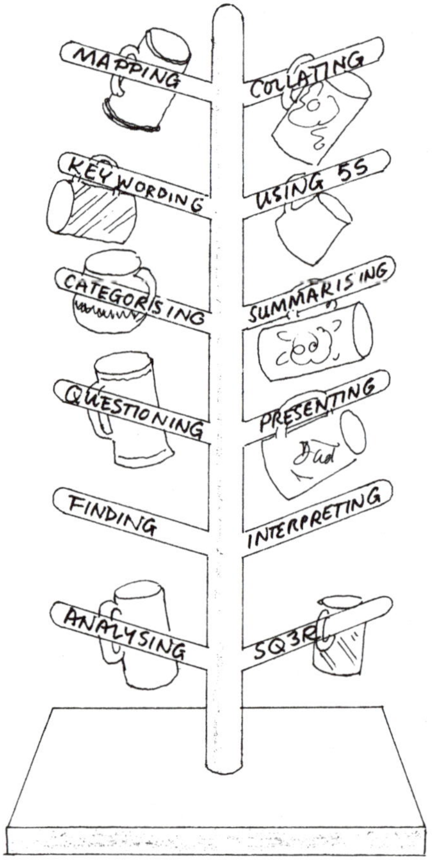

REVISION : HOW?

Revision provides the mental pegs on which you hang your knowledge.

- Revision does not involve having to learn yet more new techniques. Revision is the most important forum in the study process for putting into practice many of the strategies and techniques introduced so far.

  The point about revision as a regular habit is that if you *know* you are going to be forcing yourself to reconstruct things at the end of the day/week/month, you tend to listen better, make better notes and go halfway to helping yourself to make your end-of-the day/week/month task more tolerable. So, like many of these techniques, the act of making the process conscious is part of the *how*, the technique itself.

- Secondly, the way you *structure* the whole context of your learning with your planning sheets, time sheets, Learning Diary, and daily, weekly and monthly revision and self-appraisal sessions is an integral part of the technique of making revision a habit. So, the essence of revision is re-looking at something regularly to fix it on pegs in your mind.

If you use *skills* such as mapping, grouping, categorising and labelling, key wording, diagramming, framing questions and hypotheses, assembling clues, collating and organising the evidence, *revision becomes quick and easy.* If you don't, you end up re-reading and re-reading endless screeds of shapeless notes and photocopies, with a mind like a lump of suet!

It is useful to harness these skills to a formula, however. On p. 61 the SQ3R study formula was introduced. This is probably what you need if you are studying in depth, for instance just before an exam, because by the time you have *s*tudied the text, *q*ueried it, *r*ead it again, *r*ecited the main points and *r*eviewed it to check yourself, you should really know it well.

For regular daily, weekly or monthly revision, use the *5S formula.* The fact that it sounds like toothpaste is fortuitous as this may provide the mental association with regular application, like brushing your teeth. The 5S formula is explored in greater depth in Section 6, along with other essential skills for effective revision, such as making effective notes and organising them well. In brief the 5S formula means:

1. *Scan* the whole text (chapter, notes briefly); try to map or diagram an overview.
2. *Skim* read it, highlighting significant parts as you go, or noting page numbers on your map.
3. *Select* by using these prompts what you really need to *study.*
4. *Slurp* these bits, using a recipe such as SQ3R to make sure you can *articulate it.*
5. *Summarise*, using your map and making notes from your notes.

THE 5S FORMULA

The *5S formula* is explained in more detail in the next section because it is essentially a reading and notemaking technique. It enables you to anchor what you read, study, hear, discuss, note.

SUMMARY

Although *environment* and *time* (when you are relatively fresh and able to concentrate) are important, study *skills* will only become study *habits* (and, as such, relatively painless) when you practise regularly within a planning framework which you develop around the way *you* work best, and your constraints.

The two key concepts behind turning study skills into study habits are:

PLANNED
REGULAR

You *plan* your learning on a *regular* (daily) basis, and include *regular* (daily, weekly, monthly) rapid *revision* in your *planning*.

Reading Skills

- HOW CAN I MAKE SURE THAT WHAT GOES IN STAYS IN?
- HOW DO I COPE WITH TOO MUCH READING?
- HOW DO I READ FASTER?

OVERVIEW

Many people emerge from school convinced that it is somehow more worthy, and proof of the seriousness of their study intentions, to read slowly, to read the whole book and try to absorb it all in one thorough reading.

- There is absolutely no truth in this myth. Reading slowly is not necessarily more beneficial, more efficient or more virtuous than reading like a vacuum cleaner, just as there is no virtue in using a broom instead of a vacuum cleaner just because it is slower! Reading fast is not cheating, it is *clever!*
- The best type of reading is *flexible* reading: to be able to adjust your speed to your need.
- Reading fast, scanning and skimming and speed reading require *just* as much concentration and effort as slow reading. It is not lazy, but *efficient.*
- It is better to read something difficult through *twice* reading *fast* than it is to read it once slowly in the hope that it sticks. It won't!

Try to think of reading in terms of clothing. You choose what you wear according to the conditions — the weather, the formality of the occasion, your mood. Similarly you choose a reading style to suit the conditions — what you need to get out of the reading.

If you want to get a broad overview of a topic, you choose a very different type of reading style from that which you adopt when you check a tenancy or hire purchase agreement you are about to sign.

Whatever the occasion, there's not much point in reading anything unless you remember what's important in what you read.

This section gives practical hints which show you how the familiar skills, mapping etc, can be used to help reading flexibility, recall and speed, and expands on the *5S formula* introduced in Section 6.

HOW CAN I MAKE SURE THAT WHAT GOES IN STAYS IN?

START

First ask yourself, *'Why* am I reading this? What is the *purpose*? What do I expect to be able to know/do as a result of this reading? i.e. think about your reading in terms of *outcomes*.

- I want to learn it — commit it all to memory...
- I want to get the gist of it — a broad overview...
- I want to support my argument — get evidence...
- I want to find out what happened next...
- I want to be able to answer an exam question on the topic...
- I want to refresh my memory, revise it...
- I want a range of opinions on the topic...
- I am hunting for concrete facts and figures...

Whatever your reading purpose, you need something better to function as a *filter*, like a pair of sunglasses, between you and the text. Don't forget that text is not necessarily print. You can read a video, a picture or a map. The filter principle is the same whatever material you process. The filter is provided in a number of ways using the skills we have covered previously:

1. **MAPPING, DIAGRAMMING.**

2. **CATEGORISING, KEY WORDING.**

3. **QUESTIONING, HYPOTHESISING.**

You use the skills by harnessing them to the 5S formula.

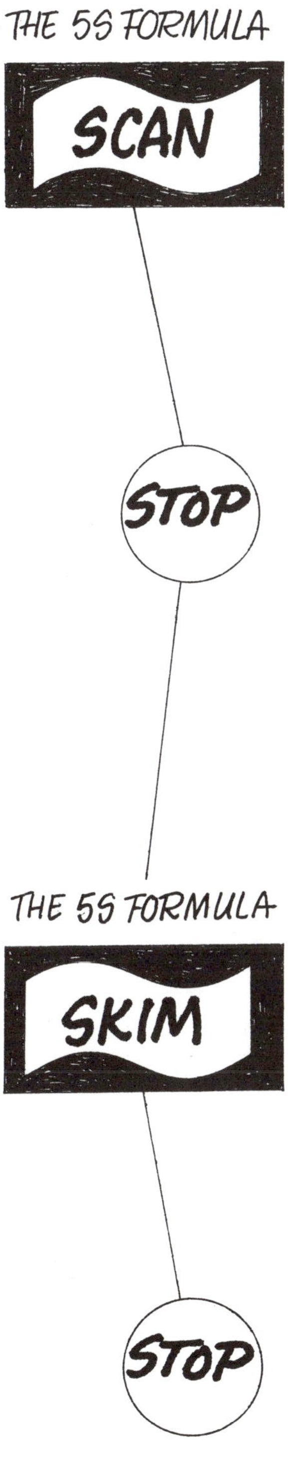

Start by *scanning* the whole text. If it is a book, this means cover, blurb, contents, chapter headings, illustrations, diagrams, captions and introduction.

After this you should be able to see the scope of it on a map in your head. *Put it down on paper* using the spidergram, lineargram or any other technique. Spidergrams are good when you read because they allow you to put the topic in the middle and build the spidergram as you go, categorising and inserting key words/terms/labels as they leap out at you from the text (see p. 50).

The words/labels/key terms which you enter into your map are what you train your eye to look for as you vacuum through the text. They form the filter.

Before you go on you need to *stop* and write down, in the form of questions, what you think you need to know from this text. You write questions because, from now on when you read, you try to see yourself as an interviewer, putting questions to the text and getting answers.

The concept of interviewing the text is a useful one to internalise — seeing yourself as an interviewer getting specific answers from a person, a book, a film or a diagram.

When this framework or filter of map,key words and questions is fixed in your head (make sure it *is* fixed in your head by shutting your eyes and redrawing it on your mental TV screen) then you get on with the next S. This may seem slow and cumbersome, and it will certainly take time when you start, but it *does* get quicker with practice, and becomes almost instinctive! Eventually this stage should take no more than 20 minutes.

You have already scanned the whole text, and you will have some idea of where the gold nuggets are! Now skim the text by vacuum reading it. This does *not* mean that you start at page one and try to read it all as fast as you can. You learn to skim at different speeds.

Slow skim the bits your scanning has already indicated might be important, and fast skim or glide over the padding. If you are reading a book, skim chapter by chapter.

Skim the introduction, the first and last sentence of each paragraph and the conclusion so that you get the gist of the whole chapter fast. If anything looked particularly valuable, go back to it and skim it again.

This should be enough to tell you whether a quick flick is enough, or whether this is going to be a bit you select for a syllable-by-syllable slurping! Again, it depends on what you are reading, but you shouldn't need more than 10 minutes to skim an average article or chapter. Often

you will have gleaned enough already and need to go no further.

Stop again! Use your *map*, *key words* and *questions* to focus the next stage, *selecting* what you are going to slurp in depth. The last thing you want to do is waste your mental batteries by in-depth reading what is not absolutely necessary. Your questions are what focuses your selection. Skim again, *fast*.

This time as you vacuum at top speed, jot down page numbers, or use 'Post it' pad stickers to mark important sections that seem to you to have something to say about the questions you are asking.

At any stage of your reading, the skimming, the selecting, the slurping or the summarising, it is this filter of key words/concepts and questions *that will anchor the text in your mind* irrespective of the speed of your reading.

Now work your way through the sections you have marked, noting down any main points *in your words* as you go, and writing the relevant key word in the margin (see notemaking suggestions in Section 8). Slurp read, but not too slowly. If you are having difficulty understanding it, read it through twice instead.

When you have finished slurping a paragraph or section, *stop* again and cast an eye over your map and key words. Did the information you noted answer any of the questions, contribute any facts, concepts to any of the sections or categories on your map?

Finally it is time to *summarise* briefly what you have read. To do this you use the map, key terms, questions and the notes you have made as you slurped. At most you spend an extra 10 minutes writing a point-form (one or two line staccato words, no flowing prose!).

You are doing this because you want to avoid reading the original material again, so when you revise this material at the end of the week and month, what you have written should be enough to trigger your memory.

Obviously, if you are studying something where you have one or two set texts you will want to return to the texts a lot more, but the principle of reading them in this way still applies.

Accept that you are highly unlikely to retain all that much of your first reading *whatever* you do. You really need to read a text at least twice before it starts to sink in. This is why two quick reads using the 5S formula and map, key words and questions as prompts and pegs will be better than one slow read, with or without prompts.

Your mind and eye start to 'own' the text when you have been through it several times by scanning, skimming and slurping alternately, and stopping to check your map, key words and questions. And finally you make it yours by summarising it in your own words.

HOW DO I COPE WITH TOO MUCH READING?

The succinct, but not particularly helpful answer is by doing more with less!

The terms 'the information explosion', 'the paper war', 'the information society' have become everyday cliches. What they mean, in fact, is that there has been a *reading explosion.*

Ask yourself *why* you need to read this. If it isn't easy to answer, why are you wasting your time? If you have a reading list do not start at the top and think that you will work your way through it.

- Try to find one or two *major* texts (in university libraries they will often be on the equivalent of 'closed reserve' or 'desk loan').

Look at the authors who are most frequently cited in the references at the end of the chapters, in the bibliography or in the introduction. *Scan* material until you have a reasonable who's who, and start by reading the work of these gurus. You can always find more obscure authors and texts later if you have time.

- Check the date of the article or book. If it isn't recent, why read it? Even history and literary criticism date!

- Learn to look for the publisher's imprint (on the back of the title page) and you will soon get a feeling for who publishes solid stuff and who does the more marginal frothy fillers.

The answer is not to read more, but

- to read more selectively
- to read faster
- to make conscious use of reading prompts and props.

There are three basic rules:

- Apply the 5S formula, and choose with great care what you are going to spend your time slurping syllable by syllable!

However uncomfortable it feels in the beginning, *force* yourself to do the 5S routine fast by setting yourself a time limit.

- *Work out a contract with yourself:* Five minutes to scan this chapter; five minutes to skim. There are five chapters so I'll finish the book in under an hour, have a break and do it again.

- If you have a tame partner you can practise by saying 'Give me five minutes. At the end of five minutes you take the book and I'll tell you roughly what it's about. Then I'll do it chapter by chapter.' One evening spent with a friend and a book in this way and you'll both understand speed reading better at the end. It is also an ideal way of tackling revision if you can arrange to work with someone who is doing the same course.

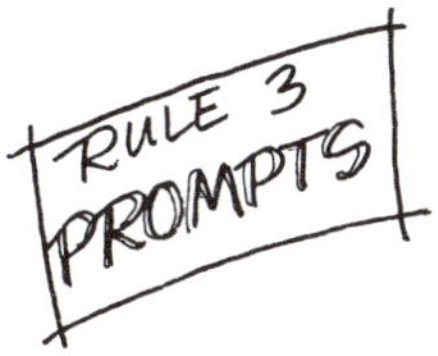

Never assume that you can do without the prompt of a mental map, key words and questions. Without them and the 5S formula your speed *will* increase, but you will spend a lot of time vacuuming up information not necessarily relevant to the purpose of your reading.

What these prompts and formula stages do is to force you to keep in the forefront of your mind that you are doing this reading for a purpose — to produce something, whether it is an essay or a research paper. The prompts help with the fifth S — to summarise in your mind and on paper what you have just read. This is what provides the anchor.

■ HOW DO I READ FASTER?

The eyes are nothing but fancy muscles, and, like any muscles, you can train them to perform faster and better!

It sounds strange, but it is a graphic description of what you need to learn to do:

Shunt your eyeball along the page!

1. Focus on the end of the line by holding your finger at the right-hand side of a block of text and running your eye down it fast, trying to get your eye to take in a whole line at a glance. You won't at first and in fact you won't ever take in a whole line in one eye span, but if you work at it, you'll be amazed at how little effort is required to zoom a line.
2. Use the scanning devices mentioned previously and, in particular, read the first and last sentences of a chapter or paragraph and then fast forward the middle bit.
3. Replace the end-of-line finger with a similar middle-of-line technique for this gap-filling type of reading. It feels less disconcerting to run your finger down the middle of the text because your eye is already 'centred', having read the first and last lines.
4. Remember that speed reading is a skill like any other — it takes a long time to build up and it atrophies fast if it is not practised!
5. Speed reading is tiring. It demands an enormous amount of visual and mental concentration. You absorb more, but only if you are totally concentrating, so plan to do it in very short bursts and alternate these bursts with slower reading or other work — making notes, adding to your map.
6. Setting yourself a time limit for a page is a good way to get started.

SUMMARY

Reading faster, more flexibly and for greater recall employs the same techniques as pegs, prompts and props in previous sections. You need to know why you are reading. Choose a style and pace appropriate to your reading purpose, learn to scan the whole text, focusing your mind on your map and questions. You need to select what you need to read in-depth, and slurp up the important bits and summarise, again using your map, key words and questions as the focus.

Research Skills

- HOW DO I GO ABOUT FINDING OUT FOR MYSELF?
- HOW DO I GO ABOUT USING LIBRARIES, CATALOGUES, ETC?
- WHAT DO I DO WITH ALL THE INFORMATION I FIND?

OVERVIEW

To do research — finding and using information — you need *information skills*. To use information effectively you need reading, listening, viewing, observing and recording skills. You need to be able to scan, select, reject, analyse and present information. All the familiar techniques are applicable — mapping, key wording, questioning... This section presents a framework for using these skills within the research process. It focuses, more than other sections, on organising the information you need for reading and study. The Action Learning research model has six question-driven stages:

1. DECIDING	• What am I expected to do/produce? • What do I know already? • What do I need to find out? • What questions do I need to get answered?
2. FINDING	• What sort of information do I need? • Where could I go to find this sort of information? • Can I find this information using catalogues, computers?
3. USING	• What do these resources tell me? • Do they answer the questions I worked out? • Do I have the skills to extract the information from the resources using scanning, skimming, key word skills?
4. RECORDING	• Can I organise my notes by indexing and filing them? • What do I need to make a note of? • Can I make effective notes?
5. PRESENTING	• How am I going to pull all the information together and present it so that the main points come across clearly?
6. EVALUATING	• How well did I do? — am I satisfied with the result? — do I need more practice with any particular stage or skill?

*The 6 stages of AL are based on a 9-step model developed in *Information skills in the secondary curriculum* edited by Michael Marland (Methuen, 1981), the title from Reg Revans' management work in America, and it combines the philosophy and features of both. It is developed in *Information Alive* and *Action Learning* (Longman Paul, 1987, 1988)

1. DECIDING

1. What am I expected to do/produce?
2. What do I know already?
3. What questions do I need to get answered?
4. What do I need to find out?

STEP 1.

ASK

- What aspect of the topic am I doing, or 'all about', a general approach?
- What do I have to produce — essay, tutorial presentation, talk, etc?
- How long have I got to do it?
- Who is my audience — examiner, lecturer, teacher, peers?
- Are they 'experts'?
- What do they know? What will they expect?

STEP 2. How can I work out what I need to know unless I've worked out what I know already?

- *Brainstorm* what you know already by writing it all down (see p. 49).
- Then sort it into *categories* and *map* it (see p. 51).
- *Label* the categories so that you have a list of key words/terms/concepts (see p. 53).

This is the most important step because it gives you the structure that underpins everything else — the terminology and approaches you need for searching for information in libraries, catalogues, and within the resources themselves; for scanning, skimming and selecting material for noting or in-depth reading and study; for planning your presentation.

STEP 3. Frame the questions you need to 'interview' your resources to see whether they have the information you need to produce an appropriate product:

• WHO • WHAT • WHY • WHERE • WHEN • HOW? .... • SO?

WHO, WHAT, WHERE, WHEN, WHICH elicit factual information.

WHETHER, will elicit possibilities.

WHY elicits causes, explanations, reasons, hypotheses.

SO elicits results, conclusions, recommendations.

STEP 4. *Plan* a *pathfinder* planning schedule (see p. 44) in your Learning Diary.

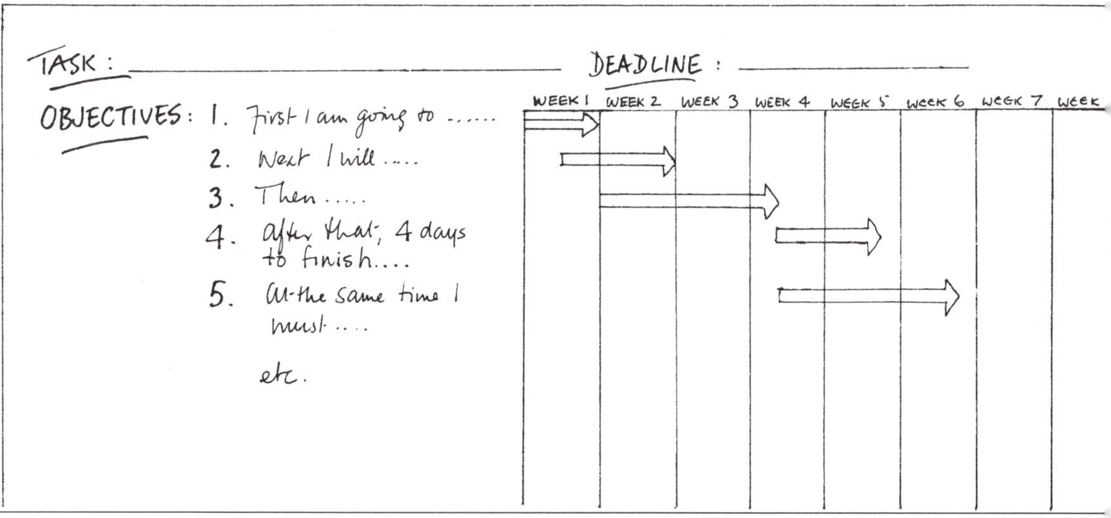

2. FINDING

1. What sort of information do I need?
2. Where could I go to find this sort of information?
3. Can I find this information using catalogues, computers?

Finding different sources of information, the right kind of information in these sources and resources: finding your way *to* and *through* the information.

STEP 1.
Do I need facts, figures, research data, opinions or evidence to support an argument or hypothesis? Do I need pictorial information, for example, pictures, or case studies?

STEP 2.
Will I get this information:
- from books, encyclopaedias, periodical articles and other print sources?
- from people, organisations, community sources?
- from libraries, online databases and other electronic sources?
- from non-print sources : TV, videos, maps, charts, pictures, etc?

STEP 3.
To unlock information sources and resources you need *keys*:

- *Community sources* keys: Yellow Pages, personal knowledge, community and business directories, pamphlets, Citizens' Advice Bureau, information offices, public libraries.
- *Libraries* keys: reference sources and services; indexes, directories, catalogues, *librarians.*
- *Print sources* keys: contents, index, glossary, chapter headings, captions, etc.
- *Electronic sources* keys: program/operating instructions, menu, etc.

Keys, especially to library and electronic sources, are becoming increasingly complex so take advantage of library user education programmes, but also ask librarians.

Most librarians *like* to help, but it is no good going with a request as general as 'Where do I find stuff on World War II?' You need to be far more specific, so you need to do your groundwork first (stage 1).

'Could you help me to find any research that might exist on the relative expenditure on armaments by Germany and the Allies in the period, say five years, leading up to the war?'

This would elicit a lot more questions from the librarian about what you were doing it for.

Then you may well be helped to look through a jungle of possibilities — specialist encyclopaedias, periodical and newspaper indexes, databases, the card catalogue for material in history, military intelligence, or yearbooks.

The more you know already, the easier it will be for a librarian to help you. They enjoy finding information — that is why they are librarians — but they cannot do your thinking for you!

Most libraries are arranged around systems with similar logic:

- *Fiction* books are arranged alphabetically by the author's surname.
- *Non-fiction* books are arranged numerically by the number code given to the *aspect* of the topic they cover. This causes much confusion. What it means is that there is no one right number for, say, horses. You will get books on horse riding in the sport/recreation number; on horse breeding under animal husbandry; on wild horses under wild animals, etc. This is inevitable. It is one of the reasons why you need to have mapped your topic *before* you start looking for information.

START

Start by making sure you know exactly what your topic *means*. If you are not sure, look it up in a general or specialist *dictionary*.

Most libraries have a *reference section* for valuable dictionaries, indexes, encyclopaedias, yearbooks or atlases.

These are usually the books you are not allowed to borrow. They are usually arranged with general material at the beginning, and the rest following the same number sequence as the rest of the library.

If you want to know what number your subject is, and what books there are on the subject, look up the subject in the *catalogue*.

Whether it is a:

Card catalogue

Microfiche catalogue

or

Online computer catalogue

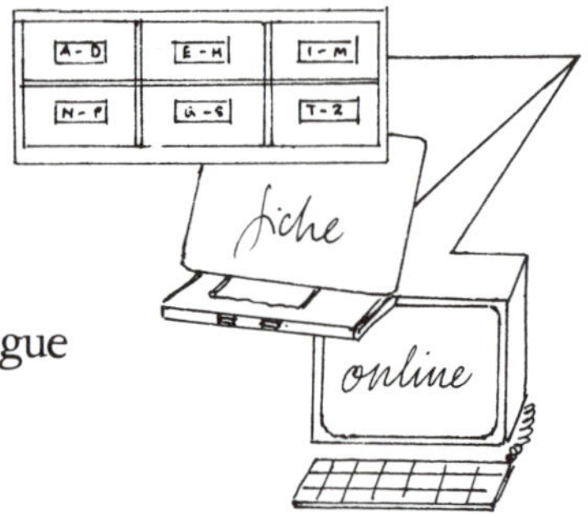

You will be able to look up

A subject,
an author
a title

and whatever you look up should lead you to a number code (if it is non-fiction).

This number signifies the book's classification or what aspect of the topic it is, and usually where it lives in the library. This example is from the Dewey classification system — the most used — but many libraries use other systems. They all work in a similar way.

The classification number (often called the 'call no') is the book's address.

7 means that it is a book in the art, sport and recreation category

79 means that it is a book on sport

798 means that it is on horse riding.

Anything after the decimal place is just a more detailed breakdown, e.g. place, time.

So, start your search by looking up as many *aspects* of your topic as you have listed on your map, using your key words, and build a list of classification or call numbers. Then you can start finding books.

If you think there may be valuable material in magazine articles, research reports or newspapers, you will need help to look up a variety of indexing and abstracting tools. Many of these are in book form (hard copy).

Increasingly, many of them are available through online computer searching. Some are on microfiche, and some are now on CD Rom (like a music compact disc, but with printed information instead of sound). These indexes and abstracts are called secondary information, because they tell you where information on your topic can be found anywhere in the world. (By contrast, the library's catalogue usually refers only to what is in that particular library.)

If you find a reference in an index to a particular article, you need to check whether the library subscribes to that periodical. If it does not, you can ask the library staff to interloan it for you from another library who will send you a photocopy. Because there can be quite significant costs, you need to be sure that it *is* what you need.

For all of this, using indexes, tracking down source material, interloaning what you want, you need to work through and with a *librarian.*

Most people think, or wish, that there might be some gigantic computer somewhere which, if you punched in a topic, would spew out all the information there is on that topic. Even with advances in computer and information technology this is still in the realms of science fiction.

Where there has been *massive* growth is in the area of secondary information — online computer and hard copy (print) and CD Rom (compact disc) databases which tell you who has written what, and usually give you a synopsis or abstract of the contents of that item.

What these databases (indexing and abstracting services, national and international) *don't* tell you is which libraries own that book/periodical/research report. For that you (the librarian, in fact) need to go to another type of catalogue index, a union catalogue, which may be computerised.

All this is intended not to daunt you, but to indicate that finding information is not a simple one-stop shop. It is a highly complex and interesting, sometimes frustrating and time-consuming occupation. You do need professional help from a librarian if you are doing anything more than a simple catalogue search to get a book or two.

For many course requirements you will not need an extensive information search because you will be supplied with reading lists and many of the items will be put aside for short-term loan. However, if you are doing postgraduate work, or even a research topic incorporated into undergraduate work, you will need to be able to retrieve a wide range of information from a wide range of sources, and increasingly, the keys will be specialised electronic computer-based systems.

Whatever your topic, whatever the level you are working at, the basic principle remains the same: The more specific you can be about what you are looking for, the more likely you are to find it.

3. USING

1. What do these resources tell me?
2. Do they answer the questions I have worked out?
3. Do I have the skills to extract the information and *use* it?

Does my information tell me what I need to know?

ASK IT!

Select carefully what you are going to spend your time processing (see p.80). Select resources in the light of your information needs shown on your information map and categories.

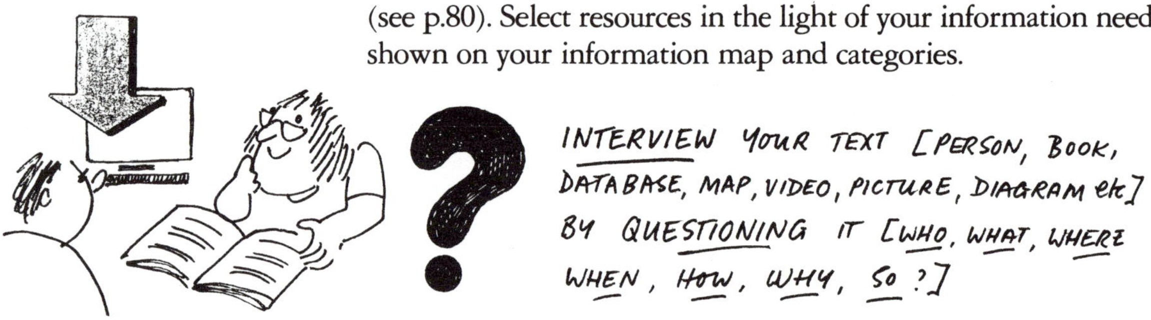

Have I got the skills to extract the information? If you can use the *5S formula* you have!

Can I analyse and interpret what I see and hear?

This is where your *thinking skills* (see Section 5) are invaluable tools, particularly

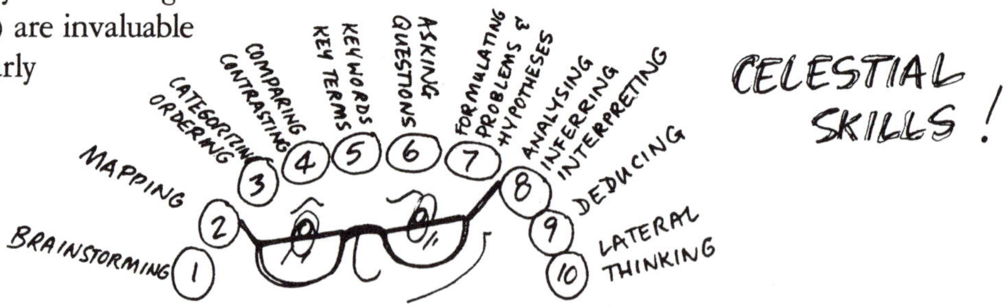

4. RECORDING

1. What do I need to make a note of?
2. Can I make effective notes?
3. Can I organise my notes?

Because making and organising notes is what many people find difficult, the following section is devoted to it. This portion summarises notemaking within a research project.

How do I know what is important enough to note? This seems like a ridiculous question but anyone who has ever copied screeds out of a book knows how easy it is to copy material which might be good but relates only minimally to *your* research purposes and needs. Once again, your Stage 1 work provides the structure, i.e.:

- your map and category clusters
- your list of key words/terms/concepts
- your list of questions.

Keep them next to you and refer to them constantly. Do not just *assume* that having done them they will automatically guide you. It is a far more conscious checking process than most people allow.

Making effective notes is subjective, but there are some basic helpful hints.

1. Use your own words where possible. If you want to copy a quote, make sure you copy it accurately, enclose it in speech marks, and indicate exactly what page you found it on.
2. Before you take notes from a book *always* write author (surname, initials), title : subtitle, place of publication, publisher, date of publication because this is what you will need for your referencing/bibliography.
3. Use tabulation, *underlining,* capital letters, c*o*l*o*u*r*s and highlighting for emphasis.
4. Leave wide *margins* so that you can add *key word index headings* later.
5. Use your *key words as headings*, so that the structure of your map is the framework you use for making your notes.
6. Don't skimp on paper. It's false economy and will cost you time in the end. Leave *space* between paragraphs so that you can add your own ideas, make links, etc.

Organising your notes needs to be done as soon after making them as you can.

If your notes are long and wordy, rewrite them *briefly* as summary sheets which you staple on top of your notes. Use your key word/term headings to structure these summaries.

Index your notes, either writing the key word terms on the top of your notes, in the margin to indicate sections particularly relevant to aspects of your topic, and/or make index cards (see p. 98) if your research is extensive.

5. PRESENTING

How am I going to pull all this information together and present it so that the main points come across clearly?

Again, this is a problem for so many people that a whole section (Section 10) has been devoted to it. Effective presentation of information hinges on the use of effective communication skills. This portion is a summary of some key communication techniques you need for written presentation in a research context. Obviously, many of the same principles apply to presenting work in any medium.

There are three main things to ask yourself:

1. *What* do I want my work to say? What are my main messages/points?

2. *Who* is my audience? What do they expect to hear/see?

3. *How* am I going to say it? How am I going to use my medium so that my message(s) come through with impact, originality, clarity?

- Whatever you are producing, it is better to have a few main, clear points or messages than an army of unrelated trivia.
- You need a **structure**. The obvious source is the map and the categories you started with. This shows how a map translates into a structure for your essay or research report:

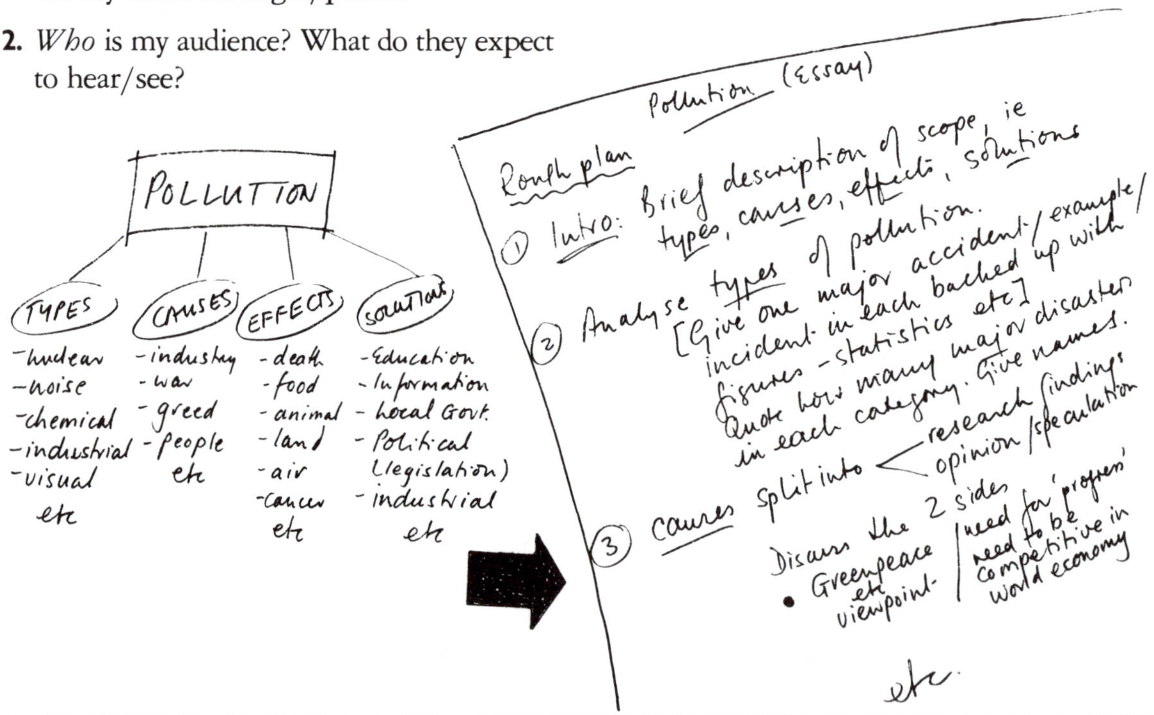

- You need to determine the **tone** of your presentation in the light of the purpose and the intended audience (see Stage 1). If I used the above structure for a research report, its purpose would probably be to inform, and I would use a balanced, factual and objective tone. However, if I wanted to use the same information for an article for a popular magazine, I might use the same structure but set out to arouse interest, shock or surprise by starting with examples of pollution and the consequences of *not* developing solutions and then add the other categories.

USE THE 'S' RULE

6. EVALUATING

How well did I do?
— am I satisfied with the result?
— do I need more practice with any particular stage or skill?

Section 12 looks in more detail at self-evaluation and self-appraisal, but this is a quick 'self-starter checklist' (reproduced from *Information Alive*)* which also provides a summary of the whole research process described in this section.

EVALUATING THE RESEARCH PROCESS

Stage 1: **Identifying information need and purpose** What did you find easy/difficult about

(1) Deciding what you needed to know?
(2) What you were going to produce?
(3) What you already knew?
(4) How to map it?

☐ 1
☐ 2
☐ 3
☐ 4

Stage 2: **Identifying a variety of information sources and resources** What did you find difficult?
Deciding on sources? Locating the resources?
Locating the information in the resources using catalogues, indexes, etc?
Were there enough resources? Right level?

Stage 3: **Identifying, locating and analysing information in the resources** What did you find difficult:

- Reading, looking, listening, interviewing with purpose? ☐
- Questioning, using 'W' questions? ☐
- Analysing, comparing, collating information under main headings? ☐
- Distinguishing bias, propaganda, prejudice, fact, opinion? ☐

Stage 4: **Recording and organising relevant information** What did you find difficult:

- Using notemaking techniques (layout, punctuation, notation)? ☐
- Working out what was important enough to record? ☐
- Using an inefficient method of recording eg, notes instead of photos? ☐

Stage 5: **Presenting the information** What did you find difficult:

- Trying to do too much, getting carried away? ☐
- Not understanding enough about the form (eg, debate) of the presentation, and not asking 'What am I doing, for whom?' ☐

If you answered 'no' or 'don't know' to any of these questions, you have provided your own diagnosis of the areas where, next time you do a research topic, you need to focus more firmly, and get help before you go on to the next stage.

*Gawith, Gwen *Information Alive,* Auckland: Longman Paul, 1987.

Notemaking Skills

- HOW DO I KNOW WHAT IS IMPORTANT ENOUGH TO REMEMBER, USE?
- HOW DO I ORGANISE MY NOTES?

People who write about notemaking often use it as an umbrella term for *notemaking* and *notetaking*. Distinguishing between the two raises some key points for remembering, using and organising information.

1. Recording information in any form — written notes, electronic or diagrammatic — is a *two*-stage process. After you *take* notes from a talk, lecture or film then you make notes from the notes you have taken. You reshape your notes using your framework, your *map, key word, question* gears, and using your own words.

The notes you make are really summaries of the notes you have collected from a number of sources. It is *notemaking* rather than the initial note*t*aking which anchors material in your head. You *make* these notes as soon as possible after you have *taken* notes from any source. This is the first step in your revision process (see p. 65). You need to do it while the material is still fresh in your mind.

2. Recording is probably a better description than notemaking because what you need to know and remember can be recorded in many ways. Written notes are only one way. With easy access to home videos and computers, learners should consider the nature of the information and the value of recording it on database or video.

Diagrams, drawings and maps likewise receive less emphasis than they should as notemaking devices.

3. The third point is that your strategy for working out and keeping in the forefront of your mind as you take notes is the same mapping, categorising, key wording, questioning process that has been the theme of the whole book.

HOW DO I KNOW WHAT IS IMPORTANT ENOUGH TO REMEMBER AND USE?

ORDERING

Notemaking is an ordering system and the point of the system is to reduce confusion by channelling expectation. Whether it is the confusion of the original raw data or screeds of notes taken from lectures or books, your notemaking serves the function of *collating, synthesising and summarising* the information.

STEMMING THE FLOOD

All of us have experienced lectures when you write frantically, trying to get it all down, and hoping that it will make sense afterwards. If, *the same day*, you work through these notes with a highlighter, underlining, summarising in your own words and trying to reprocess the material through your head, it *may* gel.

However, if you file those notes and leave it till the end of the year revision to try to make sense of them, your chances are minimal. Although it is inevitable that you will sometimes have to transcribe someone else's words, you should avoid it as much as possible by using *active listening and questioning* as a filter.

ACTIVE LISTENING AND QUESTIONING

It is tempting to assume that this just means listening harder, more actively and trying not to go to sleep! It doesn't. It means making quite conscious and deliberate use of the familiar techniques of mapping and key wording to *focus your listening* and *structure the questions* you ask of that text, remembering that a text can be a person, a lecture, an article or a video (see p. 70).

The lecture presents what is important to the lecturer. The book presents what is important to the author. You need to remember your study *purpose*, what is important to *you* in terms of what you want to get out of it. You need to:

- *Focus your listening* by using skills that, by now, are familiar, i.e.
  — *brainstorming* and *mapping* what you know already
  — clustering and labelling the concepts with *key words*.

- Keep this framework of mapped concepts and terms of front of you. You can do this literally by drawing it on paper, looking at it, adding to it, *changing* it, as you listen. When you are experienced and confident with using these techniques, you will find that you can carry this mapping/key wording framework in your head.

  However, it doesn't take much for even experienced active listeners to slip back into a passive listening mode. This is why it is preferable to discipline yourself to 'listening with paper'. This is a far cry from writing everything down. Instead it is a way of forcing yourself to filter what you are hearing/reading/seeing through your own knowledge network.

- Regard what you are hearing/seeing as a quiz show! You are the questioner or interviewer, and the challenge is to get the right answers. To do this you need to keep the questions in your mind and actively ask them as you listen or read (see p. 70).

- Remember (see p. 79) that *who, what, where, when, why* and *how* are your question triggers, the basis of fact-finding and information gathering.

  — The first and most important question is *what*? What does that mean? What exactly is this person trying to say?

  — The second is *how*? How does this relate to the concept map I am drawing on paper in my mind as I go along? Is it just the same ideas in different words? Is s/he reinforcing concepts that are already familiar, or introducing something totally different? If so, how does it fit into my existing map? Does it fit into any of my main cluster concepts, such as causes, effects, past, present, future, processes, types? Is it an aspect, another main topic, a sub-topic? Is it an explanation? If so, what is the problem/ question being explained?

- Another technique for *active listening* is to apply what you know about thinking and learning preferences to the lecturer or author. Is this person presenting the information in a way that indicates that s/he is a linear/ convergent or creative/divergent thinker?

  Do you think that this person might be a baker, presenting the information holistically, building broad, sweeping concepts and generalisations. Or is this person systematically building the information brick by brick without telling you where you're going and how it all fits together?

  If you *know* you are a baker listening to a builder, this makes it much easier to minimise the 'cognitive dissonance' (the mismatch between your view of the world and learning expectations and hers/his). You can, with practice, *teach* yourself to listen like a builder, baker, boffin or butler.

  When (as a baker) I realise that I am listening to a builder or boffin, I make a conscious decision to try to listen as a builder or boffin would. It's a bit like speaking a foreign language. It feels uncomfortable at first, but better when you get into the swing of it.

- Try to use these techniques communicatively. By this I mean that you need to see notemaking as an *active dialogue* with an information source. You are not just passively writing down words as they come to you. You are *actively* approaching it as you would a conversation with a friend: 'Hey, look, there are a whole lot of things that I know, and a whole lot of things I need to know. Can you help me?'

Before you go on, get someone to read what you have just read — a solid chunk of text on notemaking — and try to map it and make notes as you go along, using the blank or half-page method. You may have come up with something like this:

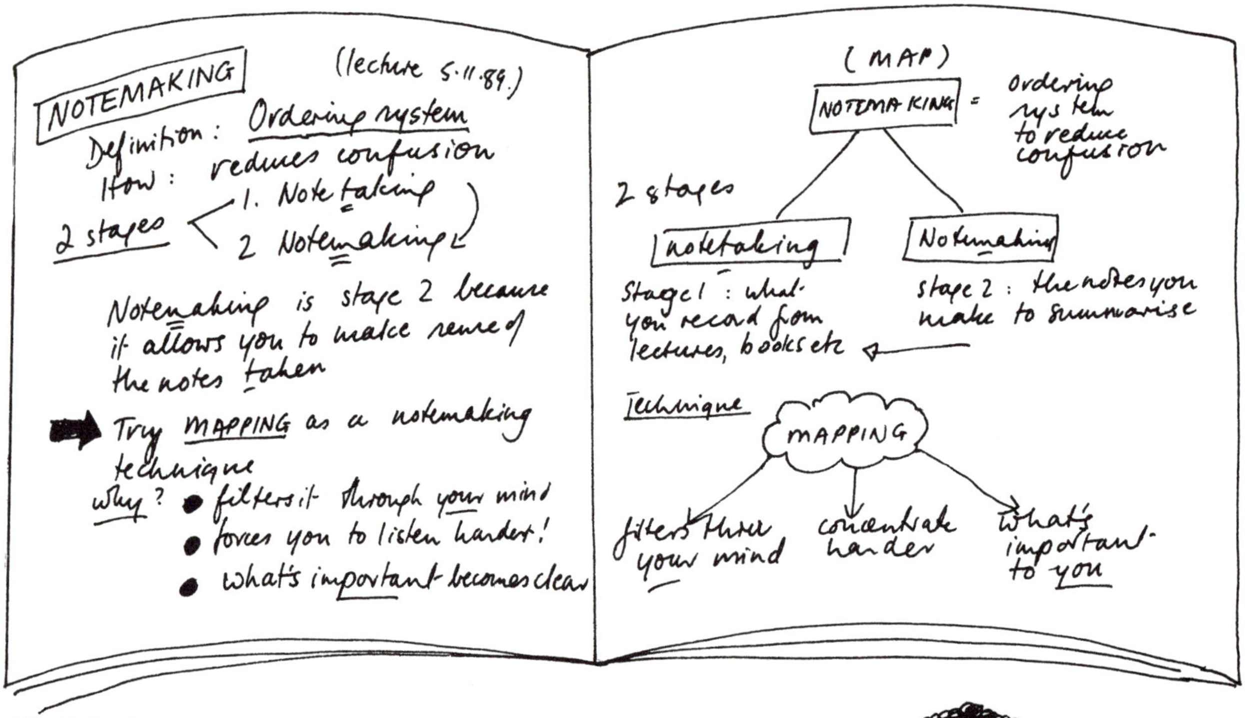

So, even if you had taken down word for word what was said in this lecture on notemaking, photocopied the whole page, or copied chunks of it verbatim, would it not be a more effective memory jog to *make* notes like the ones below, and staple them to the front of your lecture notes and photocopies?

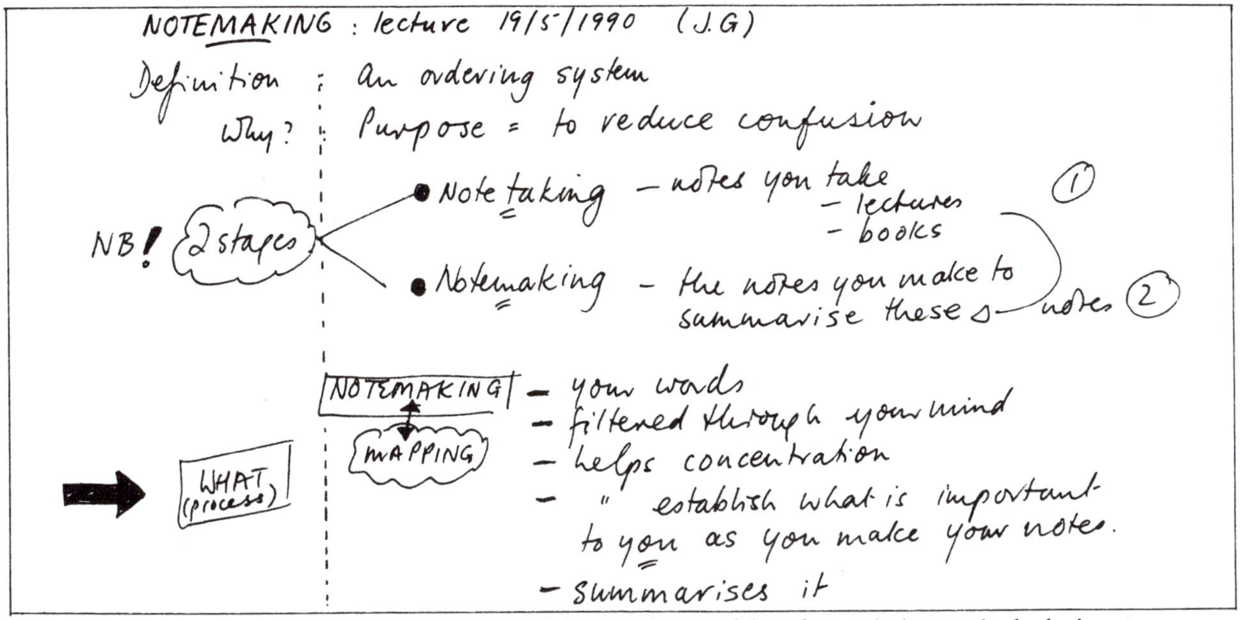

Using notemaking techniques — graphics, tabulation, punctuation highlights, emphases, capitals and other devices — also helps to condense and clarify. What you use, however, and the style you develop, tends to be a very personal thing; as a result other people's notes are hard to follow.

It also helps to develop your own shorthand. In my shrthnd it is partic NB to rem. wide margins w/out them there is nowhere to put keywrd heads, or it is particularly important to remember wide margins because without them there is nowhere to put your key word headings!

Wide margins are essential because your idea of what is important *does* change and develop as you go along. Leaving yourself plenty of white space and wide margins allows you to use the same notes every time you revise, adding to them if needed.

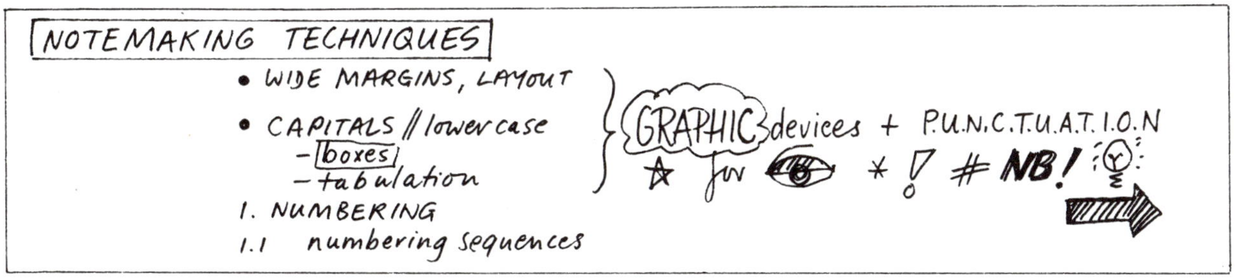

This summary has been done in the style that now comes naturally to me although I still have to battle to force myself to leave wide margins and enough white space. Look at it then shut the book and make your own note summary.

SUMMARY

You know what's important enough to you to remember, note etc

(1) by having a MENTAL FILTER through which you listen, look, read.

NB → (2) Your MAP/CATEGORIES/KEY WORDS /QUESTION STRUCTURE provides this filter.

(3) If you are taking notes on a new topic try to draft a rough map as you go.

- It focuses your listening; concentrates your mind
- It helps you to use your own words, filters it thru your mind
- Establishes what is important to you
- Summarises it — makes revision easy.

(4) If the topic is familiar, keep your map next to you and refer to it consciously and continuously to ensure that

- You only note what is important for your purpose

(+ points above)

(5) 5.1 Wide margins
5.2 Graphic devices
5.2.1 - boxes clouds * ! # ↑
5.3 EMPHASES, highlighting, colours
5.3.1 - NB!
5.4 • Punctuation, capitals
5.5 Tabulation, numbering

} Are all helpful techniques

HOW DO I ORGANISE MY NOTES?

The theme tune strikes again! You can use the same:

MAP, CATEGORIES, KEY WORDS/TERM/ CONCEPT, QUESTIONING	FORMULA

as a way of indexing and ordering your notes.

HOW TO DO IT

- If you have done regular revision, daily *m*aking note-form summaries from the notes you *t*ake in lectures, from reading, photocopying, you should have this note summary stapled to the top of your other material.
- Ask yourself whether you need to summarise even further.
- When you have a succinct one-page summary, make sure that it is stapled to the top, behind it come your note summaries, your notes, any handouts, photocopies. You may find it useful to put this top (index) summary on a different colour paper.
- Refer back to your map of the whole topic. What *aspect* of the topic does it cover? Which of your key word/term headings describes it. When you have *indexed it* (all indexing means is allocating a subject or key heading), you write this heading in the top right-hand corner. (Red pen is preferable.)

Example

If I were writing an essay on pollution, I might end up with several files, each cluster of paper having an index heading as shown.

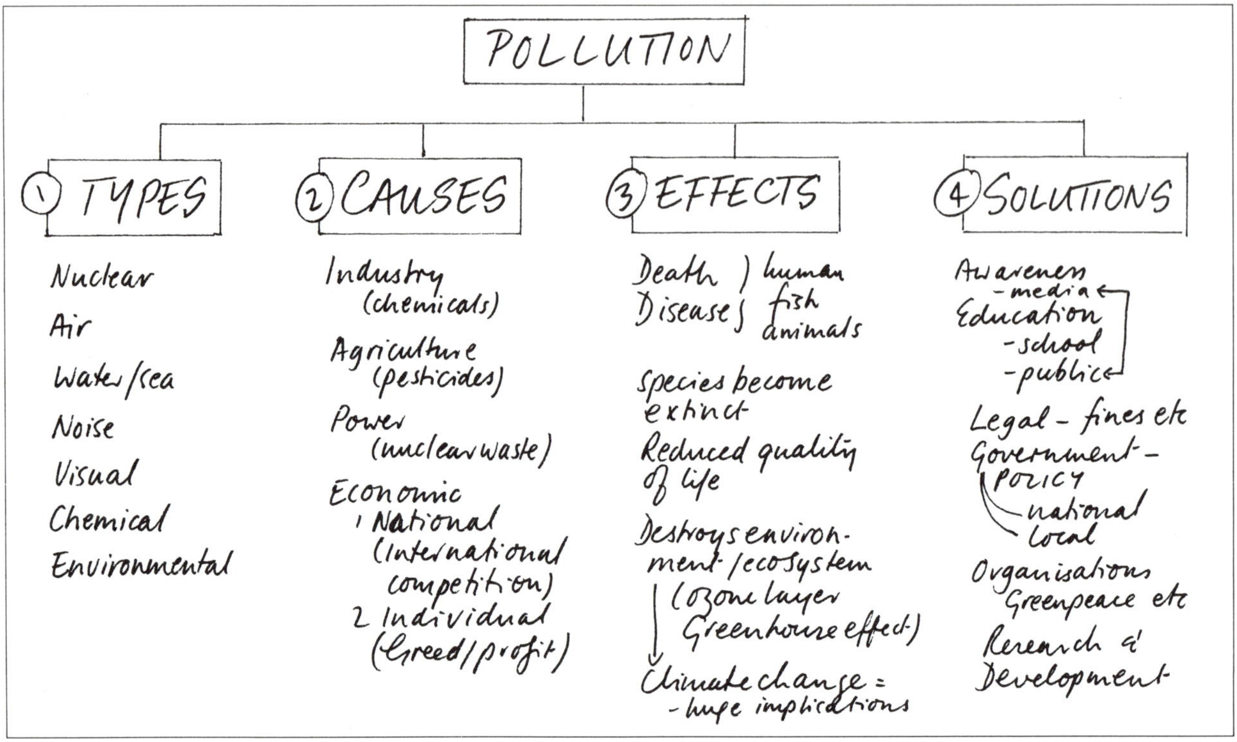

This shows how your organisation of your files, and your indexing of your notes within the files, reflects the structure of your original topic map and your work plan. It wouldn't matter if you decided to start your essay talking about the *effects* of pollution and then went back to causes, types, solutions. *Your material is organised so that you can arrange it in any way that suits the message you want to get across in your presentation.*

This is all very well, but what happens if there are a whole lot of *aspects* of the topic covered in the one article or set of notes? For instance, an article on pollution is highly unlikely to cover only one aspect, such as causes, without looking at solutions and giving details of the effects of various kinds of pollution.

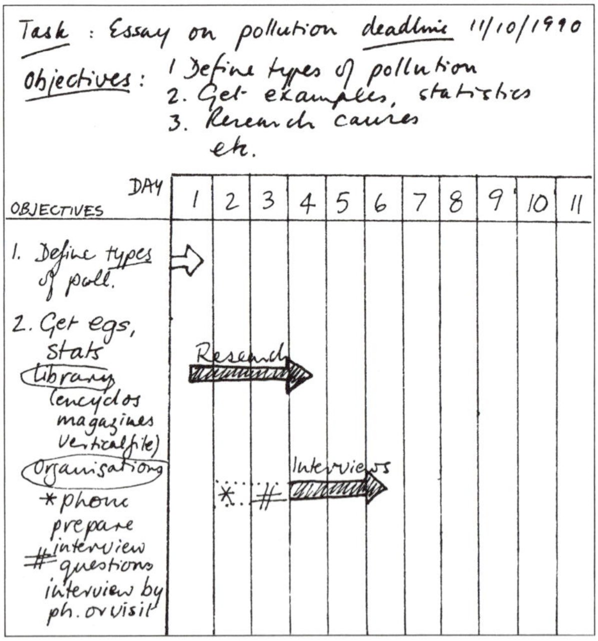

1. You ask yourself whether there is a *main aspect* or focus in this piece of information. If there is, index it in the top right-hand corner as normal. If there isn't, use the category general. It is useful to have several general overviews if you are preparing an essay introduction or conclusion.

2. This is where you use your wide margins. Use a red or different colour pen to note the key word headings for any other aspects covered in the article. So, for example, the article on pollution might emphasise nuclear waste, and you index it in red in the top right-hand corner under *pollution: effects: nuclear waste*. But it also has a good section on the greenhouse effect, and on the various organisations tackling pollution problems, so you index in red in the margin:

Pollution : EFFECTS : Greenhouse (p.5, 6)

Pollution : SOLUTIONS : Organisations (p. 11, 15)

(Obviously, to save time, you would not write 'pollution' over and over, but this is to show you the principle of indexing. Also, as in the above example, if there is anything really worth re-reading or quoting from the body of your notes or photocopies, refer to it here by page or paragraph number so that you don't have to hunt too hard!)

3. If you were doing a relatively small project, you would be safe leaving your indexing and ordering at this stage. You have given each stapled cluster of notes a main index heading in red on the top right-hand side. You have indexed each aspect or sub-topic in red in the margin. When you come to write your essay, group all the main sub-topics together in files and work from them, but you can also flick through the whole lot looking at your margin indexing notes to pick up where material in another file had something important to contribute to the aspect you're working on.

4. However, if you were doing a big project, you would need to consider using cards to supplement the two kinds of indexing described above. You would do just as you have done, but you would also prepare one index card for each main topic. For instance you might have one card for *pollution : general*, one for *types*, one for *causes*, one for *effects*, etc. Behind these you would file a card for each of the sub-aspects, such as each different type of pollution, air, environment, nuclear, sea, water, etc.

5. If you were doing a PhD you might have a separate card for each item you read filed alphabetically by author behind one of these subject guide cards. (Although I am talking about cards because they are easy to visualise, you would, one hopes, be doing it on a database, not cards! But the principle is the same.)

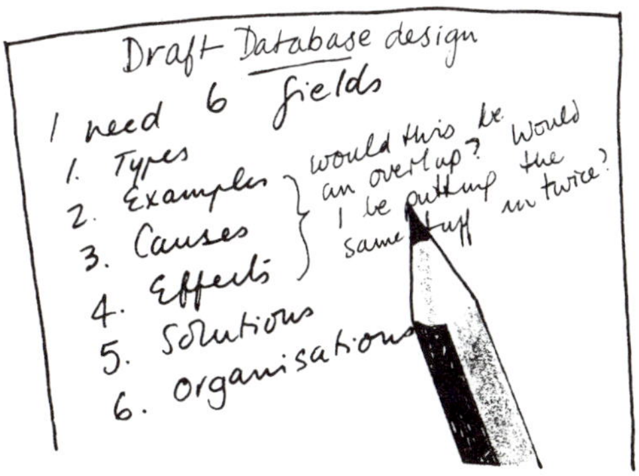

6. For less ambitious projects you can do as shown below — just use the guide card to jot down where material has been indexed as relating to that aspect.

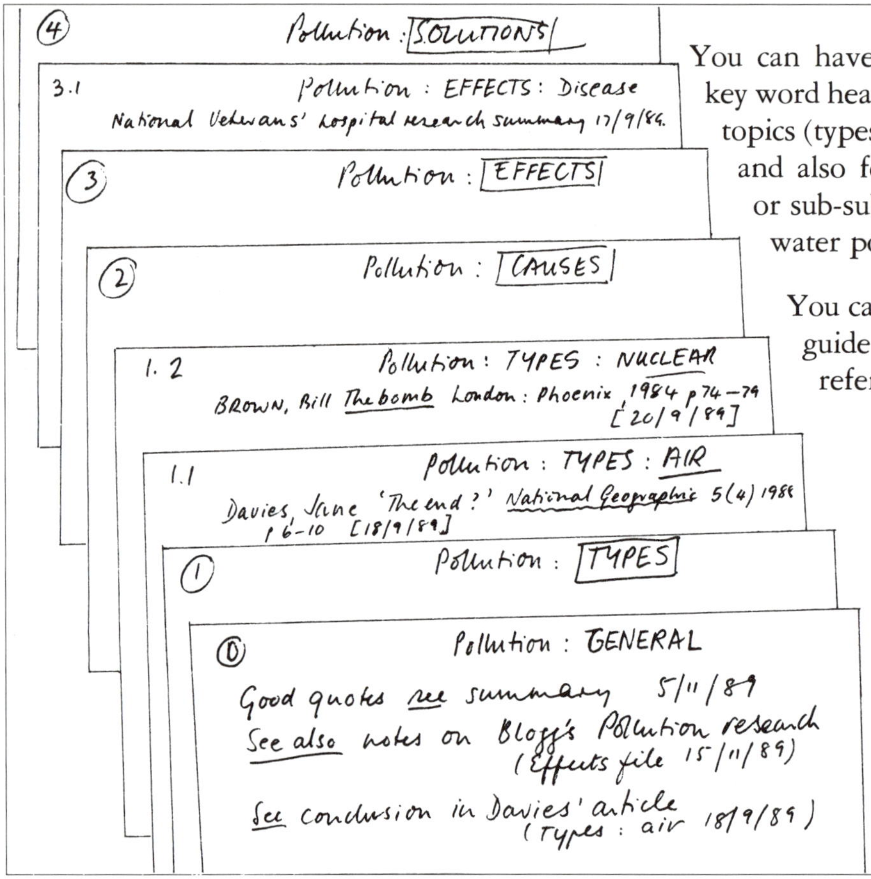

You can have guide cards (using your key word headings) for your major sub-topics (types, causes, effects, solutions) and also for all your major *aspects* or sub-sub-topics, e.g. air pollution, water pollution, etc.

You can make notes on these guide cards as your cross references.

By putting the date when you made your summary, you can file your notes in date order for easy retrieval, i.e. within each topic.

There is no one 'right' way to organise your notes. It all depends:

— on the nature and purpose of your project
— on its size and duration
— on the complexity of the topic and the material you are handling
— on the quantity of material.

However, the method of having topic guide cards with annotations to direct you to your indexed notes (stapled in clusters with summary notes on the front) which are filed by date, is a good general all-purpose, flexible scheme which you can adapt to suit yourself.

There are other ways of filing cards — having an alphabetical author index with a card for each item you have read filed under the author's surname, and doing your indexing on the card (which means a lot of hunting when you come to write the essay or whatever). Or make a separate 'subject index' like the topic guide cards, but filed alphabetically under subject, and with references to each author who has written on this topic. It can get complicated!

Alternatively, using a *database* solves many problems, because you can have a field for each point of access — author, title, topic, aspect, etc — and you can retrieve material from each of these fields.

If you have *masses* of paperwork, you may want to work out a hierarchical *numerical filing system* of the kind used in records management systems.

Pollution	1-0
Types	1-1
Air	1-1-2
Environmental	1-1-3
Causes	1-2
Industry	1-2-1
Agriculture	1-2-2
Pesticides	1-2-2-1
Effects	1-3
Solutions	1-4
Organisations	1-4-1
Media	1-4-2
Special campaigns	1-4-2-1

(This is, in fact, just another way of presenting your map and key word headings with the addition of a hierarchical number sequence that allows you to slot in more detailed material as you go along.)

If you are going to do a lot of work with indexing, you need to understand the concept of *cross references*, namely *see* and *see also* references:

1. Dogs *see* PETS
2. PETS *see also* DOGS, CATS, RABBITS.
1. This means that there is nothing under *dogs*. It is all filed under the more general heading *pets*.
2. This means that there is material filed under each of these headings.

If this all sounds terrifying, just remember that it all starts from your map, key words/terms/concepts; that the purpose is to *reduce*, not add to your confusion, so you need to devise a system that *you* understand to suit *your* needs. Whatever you do, you need to simplify, shape and summarise in the form of notes (maps, diagrams, etc) so that you can use your notes, not your original material, as much as possible.

SUMMARY

Start with your *map, key words, questions* and *plan.*

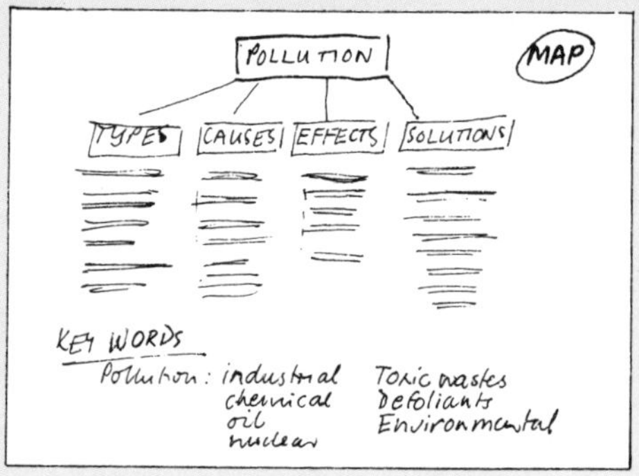

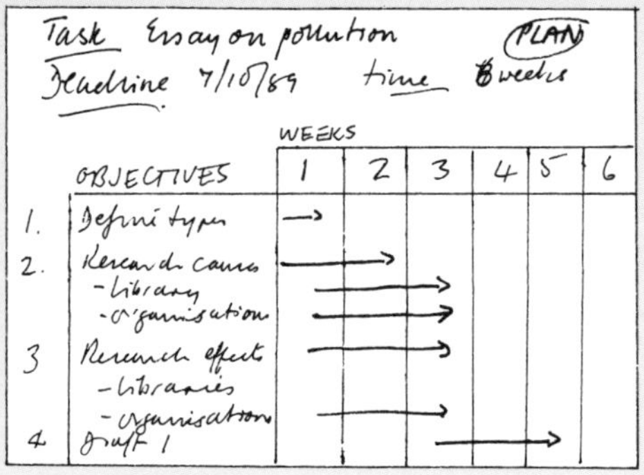

Using these as pegs, or filters, you take notes

and from the notes you have collected, you *make* summary notes which you staple onto the front of this cluster of notes on the one aspect of your topic.

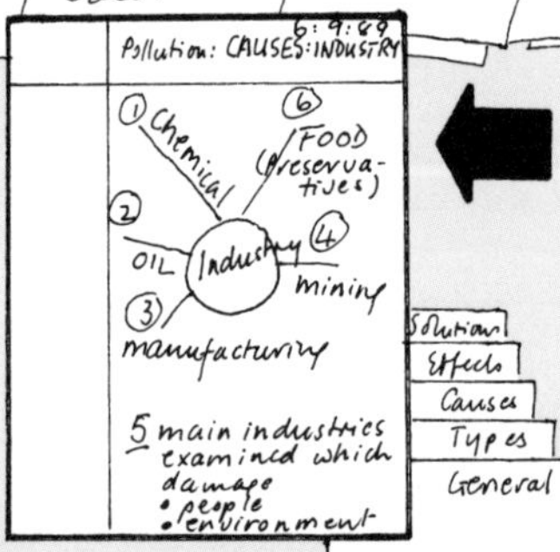

Then, using your map/key word headings you index your cover summary — top corner and in margins in red. You may also make card index guides...

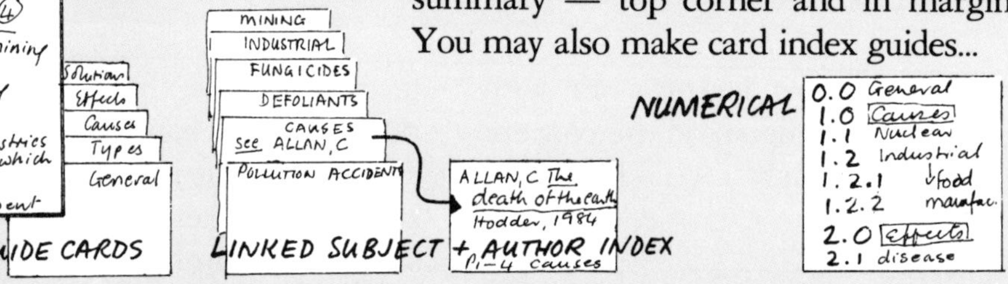

The simplest is topic guide cards using your map structure.

For big projects you might make a linked subject and author index, filed alphabetically. Or you may use a numerical system. This would be enough to get you through a PhD or writing a book. Stop where *your need ends*, but, whatever you are working at, try to use a database program on any home computer. If you design your fields carefully to reflect your topic breakdown, access is a breeze by comparison with manual indexing and filing methods.

Presentation Skills

- ■ CAN I SHOW WHAT I KNOW?
- ■ HOW CAN I PRESENT IT
  - ☐ in writing — essays, research reports, exams?
  - ☐ visually — in charts, diagrams, etc?
  - ☐ verbally — in talks, tutorial presentations, etc?
  - ☐ multi-media presentations?

OVERVIEW

Once again you use the multi-purpose *mapping/key wording/questioning* structure which has helped to:

1. Clarify where you are going and what you need to know,
2. Locate sources and find information in resources,
3. Use the information — analyse and interpret it,
4. Record and organise what you need to remember,

provides the scaffolding for communicating what you know clearly. Whether you want to produce information in *written* form, *verbally, visually* or in a *multi-media* presentation, you work around this scaffolding. Why?

a) It has an inherent logic, because it starts from the beginning when you ask 'Why am I doing this? My purpose? What is it for?'

b) It has given focus to your listening, your reading, your notes and the way you have organised your material.

c) Because of this, your job is already half done:

- — the material is organised using the same logical sequence. It is clearly structured; paragraphs and sections define themselves.
- — the material is all relevant; it relates to your questions,
- — much of it is already in your own words,
- — you have kept an eye on your questions and hypotheses all along, so drawing conclusions and making inferences becomes easy.

The essence of presentation, as it is developed in this section, is *getting your message across,* a two-way dialogue between you and your audience, whether that audience is an examiner, your fellow students, or your teacher/lecturer who is marking your essay. Presentation is *communication.*

■ CAN I SHOW WHAT I KNOW?

Irrespective of whether you are producing a written, visual, verbal or multi-media presentation, *before* you start you need to ask yourself some questions:

- Who am I doing this for? Who is the audience?
- What do I want to do — inform them, persuade them, amuse them, entertain them, shock them, convince them, show them two sides of the question, *my* ideas on the question, a general overview of the whole thing? Does what you are intending to do suit the *purpose* of your presentation, what you have been asked , or what your audience wants?
- What am I trying to *say;* have I got clear messages?
- Can I list the *main points* I am trying to make?
- Have I got the information I need to support each point?

Whatever your medium, if *you* cannot spell out clearly what you are trying to say, your intention and purpose in communicating with them, you can hardly expect your audience to do what you cannot do.

One of the main problems, again irrespective of the medium, is:

TRYING TO DO TOO MUCH,
TRYING TO SAY TOO MUCH.

Another problem in all presentation methods is:

HAVING MUDDLED, FUZZY MESSAGES WHICH DON'T SAY WHAT THEY MEAN CLEARLY.

Verbal and visual clutter are the enemy of good communication.

So:

- Write down your main points on your planning sheet (see p. 116).
- Write down your sub-points.
- Assemble your data/evidence/examples to support these points/arguments/hypotheses/sub-points.
- Check your list of questions to see whether you have answered what you worked out that you would need to know.
- See the product in your mind's eye as a shape, or preferably draw it on paper, as shown on next page.

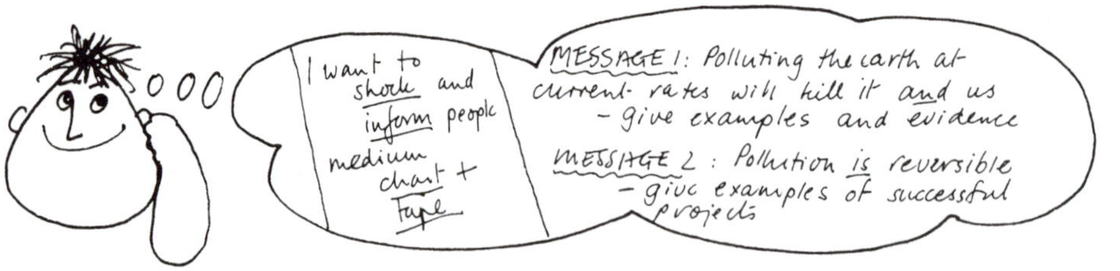

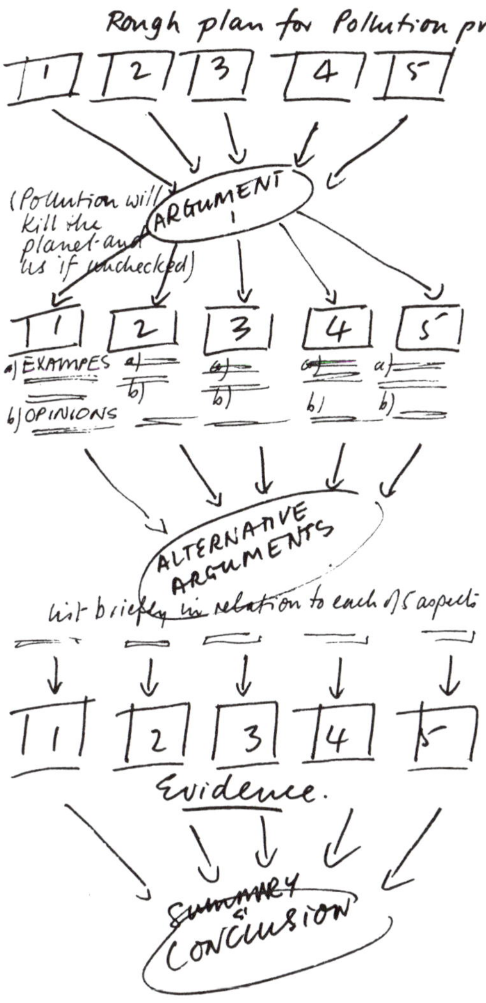

I will mention/show the five main aspects as an intro.

I will present my main argument strongly.

I will go back to each main aspect and give the evidence that supports the argument. (Try to have only one or two excellent examples and one or two opinions for each.)

I will then acknowledge that there are other views and opinions, and list them briefly and objectively.

I will then return to each of the main aspects and work through these alternative points of view saying where and why I think the argument is weak and doesn't hold weight.

I will finish by summarising my five aspects and arguments.

1. STRUCTURE IT

Return to any of the maps scattered throughout this book, like the one on *pollution*. You can see how the main topics that you have mapped (types/causes/effects/solutions) provide a built-in structure and logic for presenting the material. You can vary it. For instance, you could take one type of pollution, start by showing the effects, and then work through causes, and who is doing what to alleviate it, then going on to the next type and doing the same. You could use this to design a video, a thesis, an essay, a tutorial presentation, a chart. What changes with the purpose of your presentation (and this is determined by the audience) is the *tone* and the extent to which it is *personalised* (reflecting you and your opinions) or *objective* (factual, researched information, covering all points of view).

2. SIMPLIFY IT

Whatever you are doing, beware of being *boring*! While it is very difficult to stand in judgement on your own work, especially when you have sweated through late-night hours to finish it, you need to look for the tell-tale signs of what will bore your audience:

- Is it too long? Have you said the same thing over and over again in different ways? Have you talked *around* the point not *on* it?
- Is it long-winded and pompous? Have you used lots of words such as 'however', 'nevertheless', 'notwithstanding', 'moreover'? Check your sentences. How long are they on average? One or two longish sentences are fine as long as they are interspersed with short sentences. This gives it a lively feeling. Nothing is more boring for the audience than *long* spoken or written sentences, however well constructed, when one long, worthy sentence follows the next and so on, and on, and...
- Does your structure show through, even if it is covered with words? It should be like a well-designed house compared with a rambling add-on type dwelling. Even if your skeleton or framework is not immediately apparent to the audience, the clarity of your design is what will influence their interest and *retention.*

We have all been to talks where the speaker was brilliant, the only problem being that you could not remember a single word afterwards. What counts *for learning* as opposed to entertainment is having *clear* messages wrapped round a clear structure, using simple language with variation in the length of your sentences (written), your pace, tone and volume (spoken) and your colour and texture (visual).

Think back to the notemaking section. The difference we are talking about is the difference between a large chunk of undifferentiated prose (see p. 91) and punctuating the same information by organising it around a structure and giving it variety and interest (see p. 92).

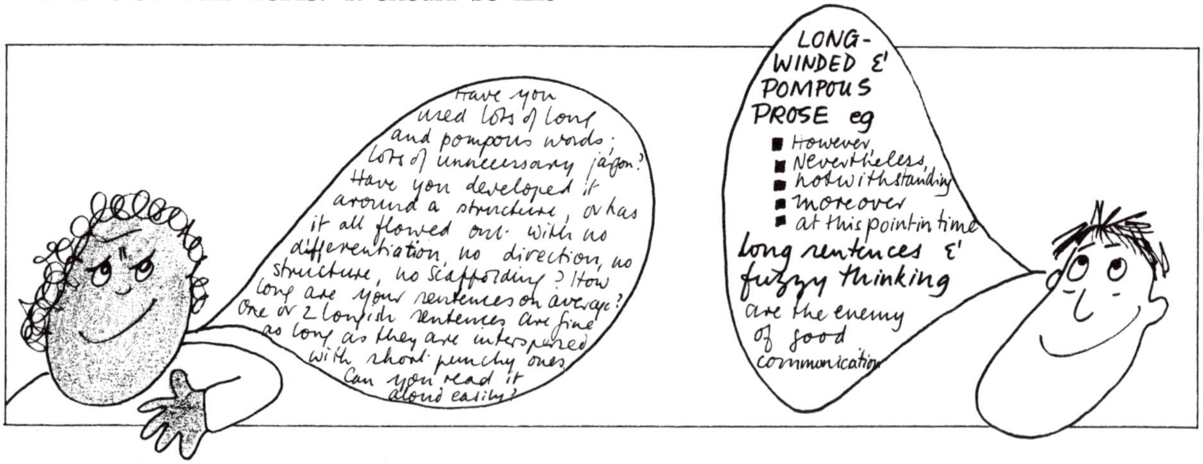

■ HOW CAN I PRESENT MATERIAL IN WRITING?

Define your terms. Give a dictionary definition or say how you intend to use a term if it is at all unclear or ambiguous, for example, 'By learning I mean the formal learning people do when they attend courses, read books, and the like, with the specific intention of learning something...'

Always do a *draft*. Structure your draft as shown below.

Work to a *structure* based on your *mapping/key wording/questioning* scaffold and *design* a presentation where the logic is visible, where it has a shape, a flow, a synthesis which will capture the interest and attention of the reader.

On p. 103 you can see an example of what I call a 'corset structure'! This is where you introduce a number of *topics*/sub-topics/aspects, follow them with an *argument*/hypothesis/theme, follow this through each aspect with *data*/evidence, and so on.

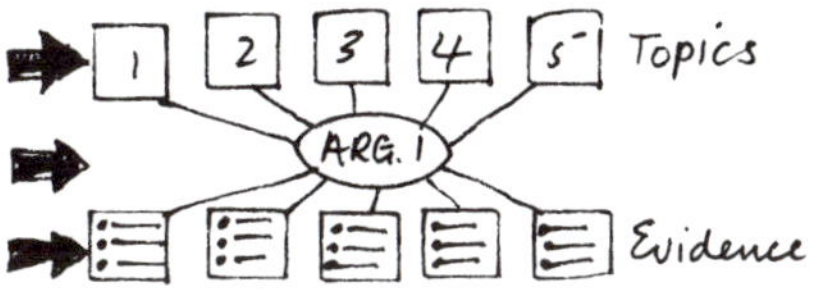

A useful alternative is the skeleton! Here the *head* is the *introduction*, — the *spine* is the *main theme or argument or hypothesis*, the *ribs* are the *supporting evidence*, arguments, data, sub-topics, the *legs* represent *where your argument is going*, i.e. your own researched opinions, inferences, interpretations, speculations. The *feet* are your destination, your *conclusions and recommendations*.

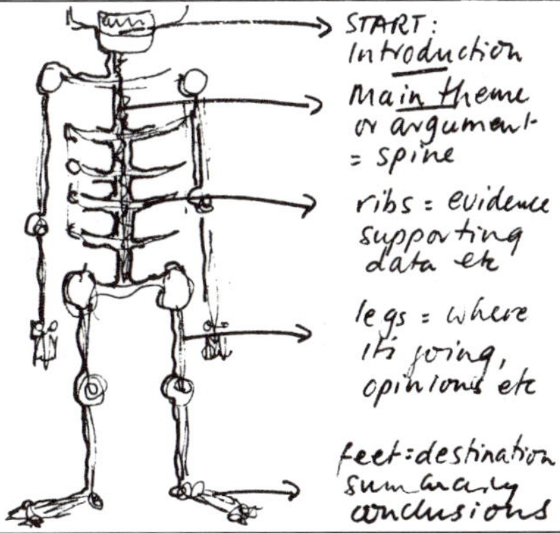

A particularly useful structure for builders, boffins and butlers who might have difficulty seeing and *showing* the main theme/ argument/hypothesis is the tree. It is easy to create branches without realising that, without a trunk, there's nothing for them to hang on to!

These structures are deliberately visual. They may not suit your particular purpose or material, but try to adopt the principle. If you can *see* a structure underpinning your presentation, your readers will *feel* it.

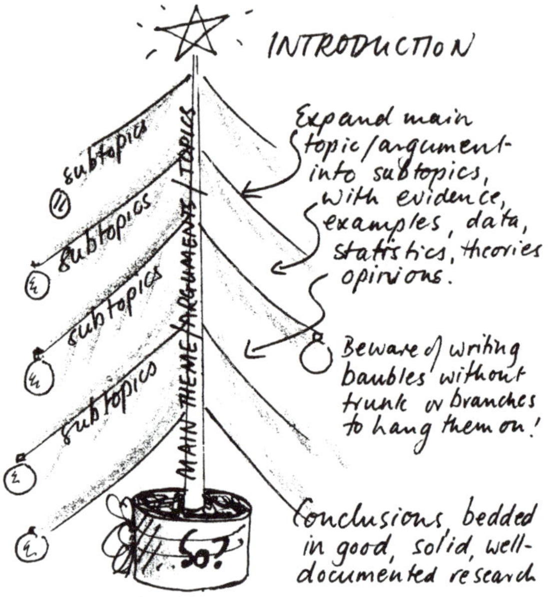

Write your main points, your sub-points, evidence, arguments, etc. roughly on pieces of paper or cards and assemble and re-assemble them until the design, the logic, the pattern pleases you.

Write out your first rough draft, using abbreviations and shortcuts - pasted in bits of photocopying and your pieces of paper or cards.

Leave plenty of space at the end of each paragraph. Some suggest writing on alternate lines. I find that this destroys the flow, and I can't 'see' the whole product emerging. I prefer to leave wide margins and plenty of space between paragraphs around my fairly tightly written and cobbled together text.

The psychology behind spending as little time as possible re-writing for this rough draft is simple. If it has taken you ages to write, you are going to be more reluctant to change it than if you have assembled it roughly to see what it looks like.

If you use a wordprocessor, you may nevertheless find it better to print out and do a cut and paste play with the different pieces before you do your alterations on screen. Especially if you are a visual learner, it is important to 'see' the whole thing as a product.

Keep the text linking your main ideas and points as simple and short as possible. Force yourself to write short sentences. Avoid jargon; use terminology where appropriate, but jargon is not to be confused with the right word in its context. Avoid tautologies and terms like 'At this point in time' when you mean 'now', and pompous terms like 'hitherto', 'whereby', 'moreover', unless you are sure they sound just right. It is a good idea to read your own writing aloud to yourself. Would you *say* it that way? Does it sound awkward?

Remember that the point is communication — for *someone else* to understand your message. Don't just *hope* they might. Don't leave anything to chance!

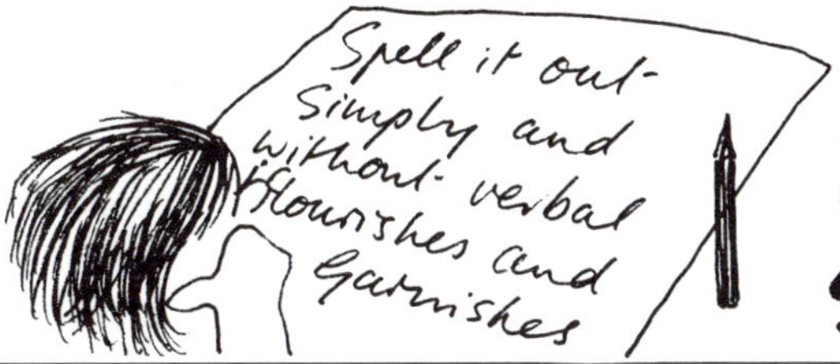

MORE **S**s!
SIMPLE, **S**TRUCTURED, **S**UCCINCT,
SHAPED, **S**YSEMATIC, **S**HORT,
SHRINKWRAPPED FOR EASY CONSUMPTION

Start in a way that makes your reader want to go on. You cannot start a thesis, a research report, or even an essay with 'Would you buy a second-hand car from this man?' but you *can* make strong, interesting and even controversial statements. Then say 'This report/essay/paper examines/develops/looks at the arguments for and against these viewpoints/arguments/opposing policies.' You do not have to dramatise or distort to make it interesting. Just think it through from the point of view of the *reader* who may well have read 20 essays or exam answers before yours and will heave a sigh of relief when she/he comes across a simple introduction which shows a clear way into the topic.

You need to consider your *ending*. Even if you have not reached any original conclusions, discovered any new evidence or unwrapped any startling revelations, you need to *wrap it up* by answering the implicit question 'So', 'So what?', 'So what have you really been saying; sum it up for me', 'So, is that important?'

Evaluate *yourself* using this checklist:

	Yes	No	Hohum
• Did I plan it using a clear structure? Could I draw this structure as a diagram?			
• Did I keep my paragraphs short, one main idea/topic per paragraph?			
• Did I keep my sentences short and simple?			
• Did I use the active voice as much as possible?			
• Did I use simple words and avoid jargon?			
• Did I use unneccessary words or repeat myself?			
• Did I use specific, concrete words, and avoid vague, woolly waffles?			
• Did I achieve a varied, interesting tone?			
• Did it sound good, read easily, when I read it back to myself?			
• Did I wrap it up neatly?			

Example

Two students attended the same lectures and handed in their essays on 'Writing as communication'. Using the 10 points in the checklist on p. 108 evaluate the quality of the presentation. Assume that each of the 10 points is worth 5%, so that 50% of the total mark would represent ??? marks for presentation. What would each student score out of 50?

Student 1

'Writing is about communicating. You must choose the right tone for your audience because they have to read what you say, so it is important that they get the messages you intended them to get in the first place. One can write for different audiences and purposes (exams, essays, books) and using different tones (persuasive, inspirational, educational, argumentative). However, one needs to ensure that the audience is never bored or intimidated, unless you are deliberately setting out to do so. It is important to ascertain where the audience is, what they know and expect from the author.'

Marks for presentation: ____ / 50

Student 2

It is not just *what* you know, but how you present it! This is the essence of writing essays, books, articles, research papers, anything.

Writing is communication. As the writer you need to think about your audience. Who will be reading what you write? What will they expect? What do they know already? Are they experts in this field, or do they know less than you?

What are you trying to do to your audience? Are you trying to impress, inform, persuade, shock, interest or entertain them? Your answers to these questions will determine the tone you use in your writing. Choosing the right tone for the right audience and purpose lies at the heart of good communication.

Marks for presentation: ____ / 50

MARKING GRID (Score 0 — 5 per item)	Student	1,	2	Student	1,	2
	Clear structure			Unnecessary words		
	Short paragraphs			Specific words		
	Short sentences			Varied tone		
	Active voice			Reads easily		
	Simple words			Good ending		

■ HOW CAN I PRESENT IT VISUALLY?

Many of the points made for written presentation apply equally to visual presentation. You need *clear points, a logical design, structure, simplicity* and *clarity*.

- Design it so that it flows, and there is some logic, some linking themes, colours, shapes and textures.
- Lead the eye in and through your chart/overhead, page/poster with a simple line

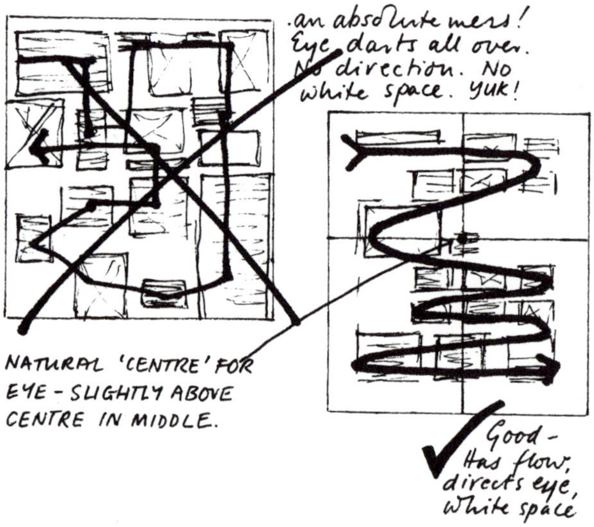

- Leave plenty of 'white space' clear areas and wide margins. Cramming material onto a page is the cardinal sin of layout. It may save paper, but it wastes the time of the reader or viewer. Presentation is all about communicating with the viewer/reader by making it easy for them to grasp your message and intent. This is no less important with visual information. Layout and white space is a major factor in readability.
- Avoid clutter. Make your points clearly and simply and have a minimum of intricate, fussy gap-filling. It might be easiest to think of it in terms of a musical composition. The music that is easiest to listen to is music with a strong melodic structure that guides the ear, when various combinations of instruments play in turn, not all at once and in different keys!
- Use *contrast*:
  - — light against dark,
  - — texture counterbalancing plain space,
  - — thick lines against thin,
  - — bold and heavy against light and spindly.
- The main problems people encounter are usually overload problems:
  - — trying to do too much in too little space,
  - — trying to say too much instead of having a few clear, simple messages,
  - — not worrying about the underlying structure so that the visual elements are jumbled and fail to tell a story, or to provide the link between eye and brain so that it makes sense,
  - — in layout, not leaving enough space top and bottom, at margins and between paragraphs and sections; combining too many typefaces and filling the space so that it looks like a visual jungle.

Example of page/chart/poster design layout.

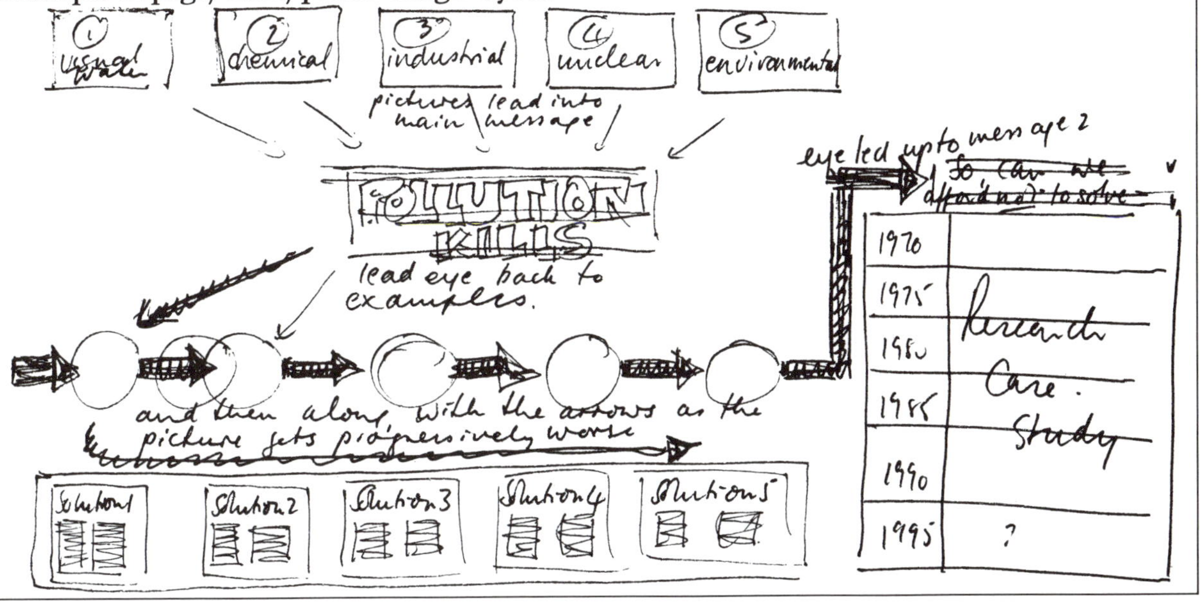

The design is based on the pollution map (see p. 96), and is intended to give main messages. The eye is led down to the first and across to the second and third and comes to rest on the case study, a solid chunk of colour and information.

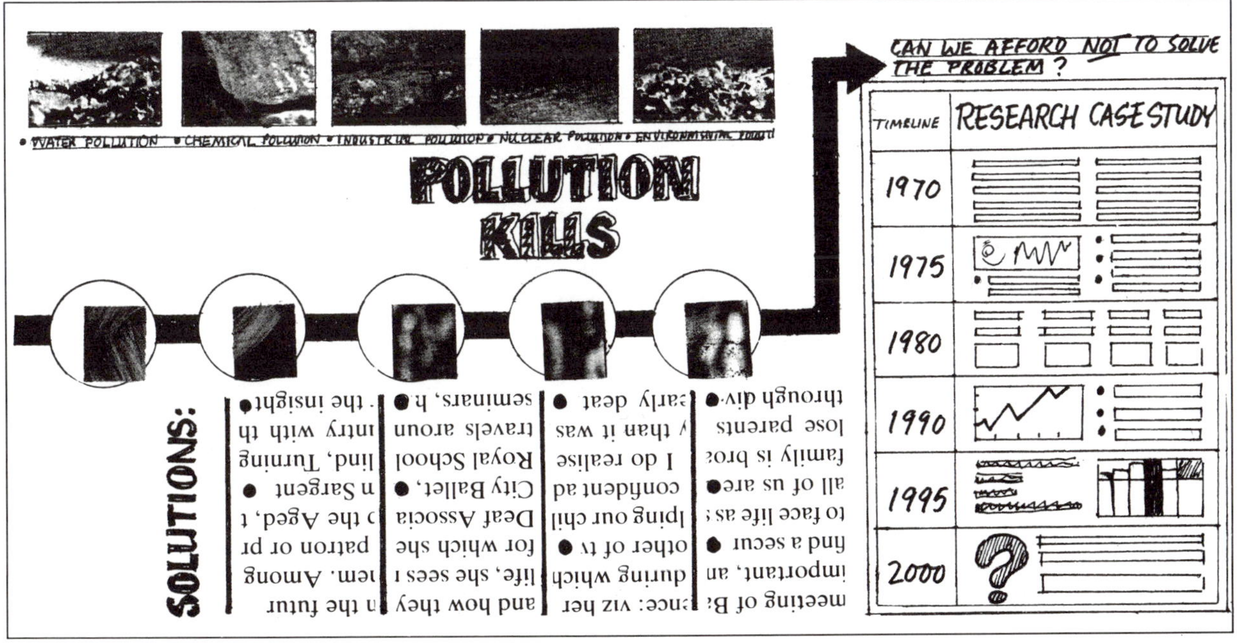

■ HOW CAN I PRESENT IT VERBALLY?

THE QUALITY OF THE VERBAL PRESENTATION DEPENDS ON THE QUALITY OF YOUR PREPARATION, WRITTEN AND MENTAL.

Ask yourself what you feel like:

- when a motor-mouth spouts torrents without pausing for breath!
- when someone reads from lecture notes in a monotone without looking up!
- when someone reads from a blurred typed overhead which you can't read at all, however hard you squint, or, even worse, when they leave it to *you* to read by yourself, assuming that you can...
- when someone waffles on and on, with lots of 'hums' and 'wells', going round in circles and never seeming to get to the point.
- when someone says they are going to talk about one thing, but goes off at a tangent and comes back with a hiss and a roar at the end (maybe)!
- when someone tries to make funnies and wisecracks or tells endless boring personal anecdotes.
- when someone asks the audience rhetorical questions, or unanswerable questions which leave the audience squirming in embarrassment and longing for anonymity.
- when someone assumes that you are totally moronic, know nothing and need to be patronised, having everything repeated till you could *scream!*

Draw up your own list of pet hates, and address them. This is the most effective recipe for success!

- You need a structure (as in written and visual presentation) with form and flow, built on the scaffold of the map.
- You need to vary pace, pitch and tone.
- You need signposts — the listeners' equivalent of headings, underlining and other structural devices.
- You need simple, short sentences, a minimum of hard words, jargon and terminology.
- If you need terminology, define it clearly for your audience.
- You need to be able to 'read' your audience's reactions. Are they interested, bored, puzzled, hostile or distracted?

- You need to be able to draw a plan and look down at it, possibly using palm cards as prompts (cards cut to fit comfortably in the palm of your hand with the main points of your talk, to jog your memory and keep you on track.)

- You need to remember that your listeners have a limited attention span. People can concentrate for about 20 to 30 minutes, but their attention peaks at about 10 minutes and declines after that. You need to allow for this when planning by introducing changes in direction, different media, different emphases (like getting them involved in doing something) when their attention is likely to waver.
- You need, even more so than with written or visual presentation, a way in that captures attention by:

— telling a joke, if you can. If it feels forced, *don't* try,
— involving the audience; getting them to do/remember/discuss something,
— telling a personal anecdote of the 'on my way here tonight' kind,
— deliberately setting out to shock, surprise, question.

Of course what you do depends on the degree of formality of the occasion, the tone and purpose appropriate to that type of presentation but the principle is the same — you need to get your audience *interested* and involved, right from the beginning.

- It is often suggested that you follow a simple recipe: say what you are going to say, say it and then tell them what you have said. This can be taken to extremes and become extraordinarily boring. But people like to have some idea what they are going to hear — like tuning their mental radios to the right station — and you need a lead-in time when they can look at you, settle down, stop thinking of tonight's dinner and get their minds focused on the topic.

> You'll all remember the story about the hare and the tortoise? Tonight I'm going to ask you to decide whether you are a hare-type person or a tortoise-type person, and which is more effective when it comes to ...

OR

> Seldom a day goes by when we don't hear about or read about pollution to the point where it becomes quite boring. It's easy to get desensitised through over-exposure. *But,* did you know the stark fact that if we go on polluting the planet at present rates, our grandchildren will *have* to go to the moon if they want to survive. This planet will not be capable of sustaining life in 30 years' time. ➧

This may sound dramatic, but I'll show you how the evidence stacks up. Then I'll look at ways we can delay it or prevent it, and who is doing what at national and international levels...

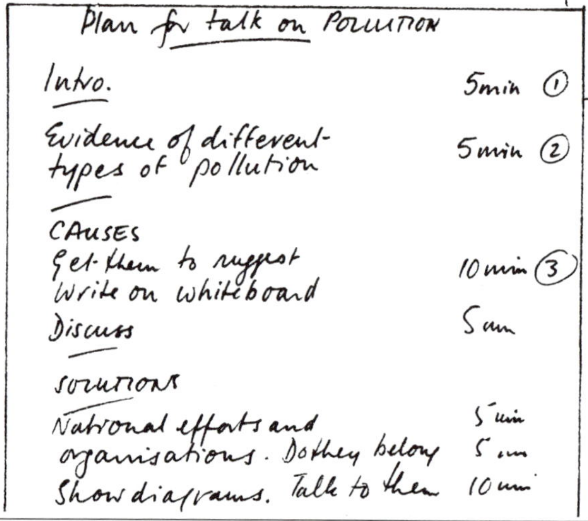

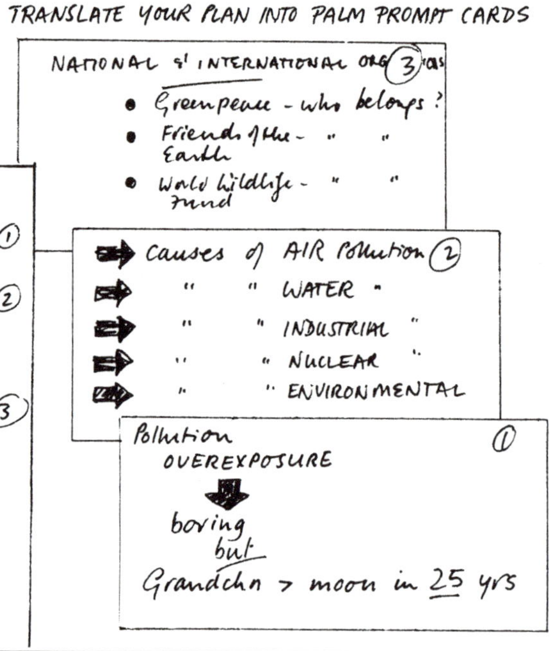

- You also need to do more summing up at various points than in a visual or written presentation. These can be casual:

  'So this is another reminder of the point I made at the beginning about our planet being set to self-destruct within a century ... , An even more powerful piece of evidence is...'

  or formal:

  'Let me now return to the main points established by the research.'

- You need to work on a punchy conclusion, summarising where you have been, but also leaving people with some feeling of involvement in and commitment to what you have been saying, a feeling that it has been worth listening to you. You don't have to leave them exhausted in the wake of a display of academic virtuosity that did a lot for you but that they could not understand, or worse, did not want to, coming away thinking, 'Well, I suppose that was brilliant, but I'm a bit thick...'

Keep in mind that all presentations are communication, two-way and potentially interactive, even in a lecture situation when the audience does not have the opportunity to question or discuss. All the more reason, in fact, to conceive it as a dialogue — asking questions, quoting well-known and controversial people, leaving your audience feeling that you have shaped something unique and valuable which has both interested and involved them and *left them wanting more!*

HOW CAN I PRESENT IT IN MULTI-MEDIA PRESENTATIONS?

Using more than one medium potentially increases impact on the audience because you are appealing to different senses at the same time. For instance, you talk to an overhead transparency while you demonstrate with a chart, as well as writing and drawing diagrams on a flip chart as you go along.

The ground rules applying to written, visual and verbal presentations still apply, but:

- Beware of getting so carried away with the gadgetry that you lose sight of the fact that you are communicating *messages* to an audience. Many computer demonstrators, for instance, can get carried away by their own expertise.
- Beware that if you use more media together, you need *simple* messages because your audience's attention is divided between looking and listening.
- Rehearse it first thoroughly. Don't just assume that it will all come together. The rule of thumb is allow twice the amount of time you think you need, because if anything can go wrong, it will. The worst thing is someone rushing through brilliant visuals which have obviously taken hours of preparation.

PRESENTATION TEMPLATE*

PRESENTING WHAT YOU KNOW

name/s ____________________

topic/project ____________________

Introduction (brief description of what your topic is, how you will cover it, the main points you will make)

____

____

____

____

____

WHAT are the most important points you want to make/conclusions/findings? (Support with evidence from your research)

Point 1

Point 2

Point 3

Point 4

Point 5

WHY?

WHEN? WHERE? WHO? WITH WHOM?

HOW?

WITH WHAT RESULT?

CONCLUSION?

This is a general checklist. Different topics will require different approaches, but it is always a good idea to focus what you do by asking: 'WHAT am I trying to say to WHOM and WHY?'

*Gawith, Gwen *Information Alive,* Auckland: Longman Paul, 1987.

Exam Technique

- HOW DO I OVERCOME THE 'THEY'RE OUT TO GET ME!' PHOBIA?
- HOW DO I LEARN TO MAKE THE BEST OF WHAT I KNOW?
- HOW CAN I PRODUCE THE GOODS UNDER PRESSURE?

OVERVIEW

How you react to exams is *partly* a matter of chance — your personality, your past experience, your level of confidence and self-esteem. But it is only partly so, just as some people *are* cleverer than others, prettier or more handsome, shorter, taller, whatever!

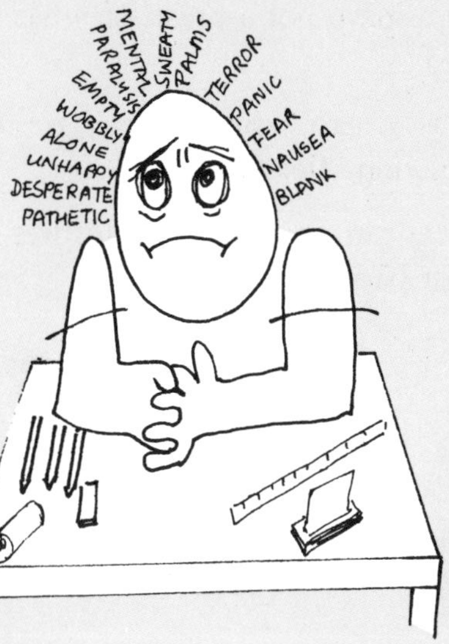

The other part is back to the Boy Scouts' motto: *Be prepared!* As they say about painting, the quality of the job has less to do with talent and personality than with the thoroughness of the preparation.

The best preparation is to have worked regularly, *revised regularly* (see p.65) by making notes and summaries (p.92), and organising and indexing your notes, handouts and photocopies (p.95), so that revision is just that — going over something you already know.

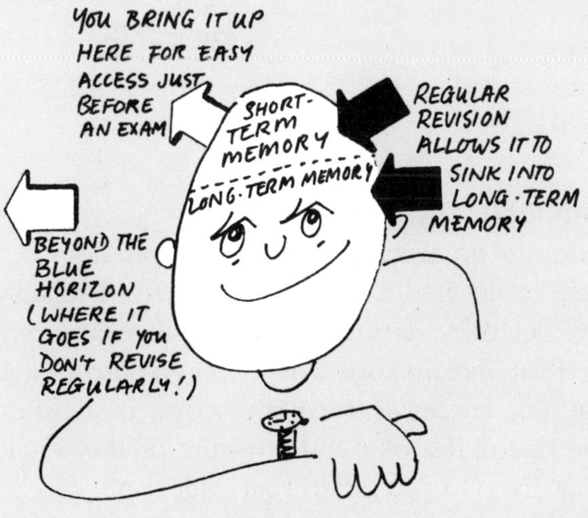

Revising something is like hauling it out of long-term memory where it has consolidated *if* it has been read, re-read, structured, summarised and anchored in your mind, and having it close to the surface to use on demand.

This section looks at ways of overcoming exam phobia through good preparation and efficient exam techniques, and links it to the strategies that have underpinned the whole book.

■ HOW DO I OVERCOME THE 'THEY'RE OUT TO GET ME' PHOBIA?

First by realising that they are not! Most examiners would rather pass someone than fail them and, really, it is people who fail themselves. All the examiner is doing is looking for *positive* evidence:

- that you have got a grasp of what you have learned
- that you can apply it with accuracy/ imagination/ flexibility
- that you can analyse and interpret material, not just parrot it.

An exam is an opportunity to show off what you are *proud* to have learned. This doesn't mean that you swagger and prance intellectually. But, likewise, it does not mean that you are so terrified of the audience that you refuse to go on stage at all! Basically the audience and the examiners are no different. They like to be entertained. They will reward a virtuoso performance but will also be quite satisfied with a performance which is dedicated, skilled and shows application, even if it does not fall into the category of sparkling brilliance.

NO ONE LIKES EXAMS!

You are no exception! But it simply does not help to develop a 'thing' about them. Probably the healthiest attitude is to see an exam as a performance. No one would ever go onto a stage without having learned the script, their lines, the dance, the plot and structure of the whole play. Even so, you can still get stage fright, freeze, need prompting on occasions, but you get over it because you are confident of your preparation.

If you are capable of sparkling brilliance you probably know it already and will not be reading this book, so assume that we are talking about good, solid *average* exam performance which gives the audience what it wants ... This is within the reach of most people. If you have done the work and prepared for the exam, you should have no trouble. If you have done less than you should have (and who hasn't on occasions!) you can *still* make the best possible use of what you know by using good exam techniques.

HOW DO I LEARN TO MAKE THE BEST OF WHAT I KNOW?

EFFECTIVE EXAM TECHNIQUE

Effective exam technique starts with *good preparation*. Obviously, as has been stressed repeatedly throughout this book, the best preparation is *regular revision* (see p. 65). You consolidate the material and make it your own as soon as possible after you have heard/learned/read/seen it using a routine of brief daily, weekly, monthly notemaking and summarising. But we are all human, and even paragons of academic virtue slip from time to time. Even if you have not done this regular revision programme, you can still benefit from organising your last-minute preparation better.

REVISION

1. Look at the whole syllabus or curriculum. Revise and map it so that you can see how all the topics or sub-topics, etc inter-relate.

2. Plan your revision schedule. Set specific targets to complete certain sections by a certain time, interspersed with other revision, exercise, treats and plenty of sleep.

3. Develop a routine for your revision:

a) Look at your map. Work out how the part you are revising fits into the whole.

b) Go through your note summaries, the *map/key word/question* frame you made for each section, and try to do it again without looking.

c) Before you start in-depth reading and swotting, get hold of past exam papers and look at the type of questions asked. Are they factual, interpretative, detailed or broad questions? Can you see any pattern? Are they more interested in a regurgitation of facts, or do they require *your* analysis, interpretation, opinion? If they use words such as 'discuss', 'analyse' and phrases such as 'How do you see...', 'your view/opinion' they want *your* analysis and interpretation. If they use terms such as 'evaluate', 'compare', 'contrast' they want to know that you can look at your knowledge and make inferences, draw conclusions, weigh up the different properties, *make use* of your knowledge.

d) Look at any course work you have done. What were your marks and comments? Where do your strengths and weaknesses lie in relation to this subject? Where are you going to make a special effort to ensure that you do not slip up in the same way in the exam?

e) Write a list of best/worst questions from the last five years.

4. Revision sessions should now feel more focused. You will have:

- an overall view of the topic
- an overview of the particular bit of the topic you are revising
- a good understanding of the type of question you are likely to face
- a good idea whether this area is one of your strong points.

If it is *not* one of your strong points, prepare your performance even more meticulously by:

- reading your note summaries
- reading your lecture notes, handouts and photocopies
- reading the relevant part of the textbook, if there is one.

Then write

Possible exam topic:	Evidence/examples
main ideas 1. 2. 3.	

Or, with your books and notes closed, re-draw the map, or in the case of a history-type topic the timeline.

DATE	MAIN EVENT	MAIN CHARACTERS	WHAT HAPPENED
18 June 1815	Battle of Waterloo	Napoleon + 72,000 troops Marshal Ney Wellington Blücher + 68,000	Napoleon I's final defeat Ney moved too slowly – allowed Wellington to retreat to a good defensive position. He then

5. When you have 'gutted' your notes and made sure that you have internalised the important ideas, facts, events, characters, then go back to the worst exam question. Could you answer this question now? If not, why not? Revise again.

6. Then take the worst question and do a mock answer not using any books or notes. Plan it, and draft it out in note-form (see below):

Question: How have developments in Information Technology influenced employment trends in recent years?

① What *is* Information Tech.? [I will need to define it]
What exact [illegible] are we talking about. [I will have to limit it to computers / CD Rom / telecommunications technologies like teleconferencing / combination technologies like ISDN / videoconferencing / videodiscs

② I will have to give a rough idea of what developed when

HOW CAN I PRODUCE THE GOODS UNDER PRESSURE?

By learning to regard pressure as a challenge, not a bogey!

You do this by giving yourself regular practice in pressure situations well in advance of the exam. Make pressure part of your regular planned revision and study by setting deadlines and simulating exam conditions (no texts, relying on your memory to complete a task in a given time).

Ask yourself what exactly makes the pressure unbearable during exams:

- you don't know enough?
- you panic in the exam situation, and, despite all your preparation, you just go to pieces?
- you just can't think clearly and you forget it, or you can't get it out although you know you know it?
- you just can't write fast enough and you never finish in time?

1. Examiners don't want to read flowery, garnished prose, so concentrate on training yourself in your revision to write point-form, skeletal summaries with a minimum of embellishment. With these skeletons anchored in your mind all you have to do is link them together with the minimum necessary to make it grammatical.

• March '89 Exxon Valdez aground • 41,000 tonnes crude oil into Prince William Sound, Alaska • 19,000 km coastline polluted • Collected 36,000 dead seabirds (Est. 1/3 of total) + sea otters, eagles, seals • US $1b. – 11,000 workers • more needed • 5 yr budget = $393 m.	In March 1989 the Exxon Valdez, an oil tanker, ran aground in Prince William Sound in Alaska. 41,000 tonnes of crude oil was spilled, polluting 1900 kilometres of coastline, killing 36,000 seabirds (although this is estimated as 1/3 of the total actually killed), plus seals, eagles and sea otters. Although it has already cost US $1 billion for 11,000 workers to clean up, further work

2. If you are always convinced that you do not know enough, remember that 'enough' is relative. There is a limit to how much anyone can get down on paper in three hours. The idea is to make sure that you use whatever you know.

If you have done broad-based revision and trial answers for some of the worst questions, you should not be fazed. People often recommend 'spotting'. It is a good idea to anticipate particular questions, and no one would suggest that every inch of the syllabus warrants the same amount of study. But if you pin all your hopes on being able to parrot one or two things off by heart, then you are your own worst enemy!

3. If you are inclined to panic, get control of yourself by setting targets and dividing up your time: 'I'm not going to think any further than the next 30 minutes and Question 1. I'll spend a few minutes doing deep breathing and really making sure I've read the question. Then I'll have a go at mapping what I can remember in relation to their question. That leaves me at least five minutes for an introduction, five minutes for each of the main points, and the last five minutes to revise what I've done and write a conclusion.'
This helps you to take your mind off how you are feeling and put it onto the task — to perform for this audience and treat whatever you are experiencing as temporary stage fright. The show must go on! When you really are panicky, forcing yourself to focus on the task, will help because it removes you one step from the situation.

4. You cannot get your mind under control unless you have your body and emotions under control. Try to get some exercise and a reasonable night's sleep before the exam. If it suits you, plan a burst-relax-burst-relax revision routine, rather than several marathon shifts, because you will end up feeling horrendous by the time the exams start.

Corny as it may sound, get someone to teach you to do deep (yoga) breathing and relaxation. This means concentrating on breathing in from your diaphragm. It calms and relaxes you. It is a good thing to do the night before an exam, and immediately before an exam.

Relax by deep breathing and alternately stretching and relaxing every part of you, working upwards from your toes and paying particular attention to your hands (shake your hands loosely from the wrists) and your eyes, jaw and forehead. Shut your eyes, let your jaw go slack, and feel as if cool, soft fingers are massaging your eyes and forehead gently. At first you feel like a banana, but it does work! It ensures that you get the maximum amount of benefit from your sleep before an exam.

5. Check, check and double check (phone a fellow student) to make sure that you have read your exam timetable accurately. It causes unnecessary trauma to thousands of students every year, so don't assume — check!

6. Plan your time to arrive at the exam reasonably early. All you don't need is to drive round and round the block looking for parking with your panic rising! Have spare pens, pencils, etc. Chat if you like. Withdraw if you prefer solitude, but relax. Nerves are normal, but don't allow yourself to get into a state. You can control it.

7. Everyone feels a moment of blind panic when they get the exam paper! It is a 100% totally normal response! But what you do next is vital. Scan it and groan inwardly and loudly, but then read it slowly and carefully, word by word, question by question. Change your focus quite deliberately from 'I don't know anything, help!' to 'OK, so what does the audience/examiner want? What do they expect me to know by asking me this, in this way?'

8. Many students know a lot, but do badly in exams because they make the elementary mistake of not answering the question as it was set. Sure, they may write on the topic, but this is not the same as answering the question.

This is one of the reasons why the question and hypothesis formulating stage of the mapping/key wording/questioning framework is such good preparation. You will be accustomed to thinking of topics in terms of self-set questions.

Questions set by someone else may be worded differently, but will almost inevitably be asking the same thing. So, instead of giving way to panic, ask yourself 'What are they actually asking? Is is like what I've asked myself?' So, do take time to read the questions really slowly, and get behind the words used to what it is they actually might want you to know and say.

9. Don't plunge into the paper. Work out how much time you need to allow for each question, giving yourself 10 minutes at the end for slippage and re-reading. Then write your deadlines down. Keep to your deadlines. If you finish one question early, go on to the next, and leave space at the end of each question so that, if you have time at the end, you can go back and fill gaps.

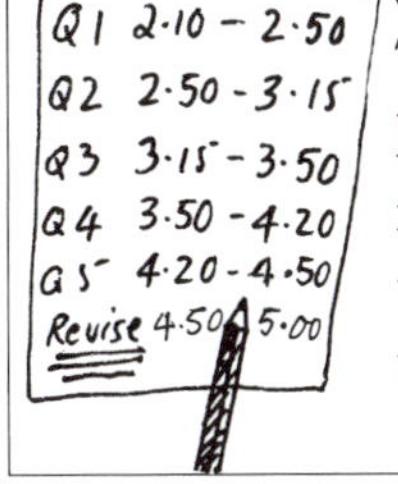

Do not over-run your deadline and hope that you can make up time on the next question. You will not. You will just get further and further behind. Learn to allocate your time according to the marks, if there are not equal marks for various questions.

10. *Plan* your answer. This is the most important part of exam technique. Use your familiar *mapping/key wording/questioning* framework, or a timeline and sketch out the scope of your answer, just as you would now do for an essay, *before* you start writing. This has two major benefits:

1. It clears your head and gives you a framework for allocating your time within the period you have allowed for the question.

2. It shows the marker that you can shorthand the content without waffle. 'Now why did Henry VIII murder his wives? That is a very interesting question to which there may well be several equally valid answers. I shall attempt here to describe...' What does this actually *tell* an examiner? Yet is it the sort of padding that frequently passes for knowledge in exam answers.

With a 'roadmap' in front of you, you can monitor your time as you go along. If you run short, write less. Unless you have been forbidden to do so, if time is short, write point-form answers (see below). It is more important to show the examiner that you know the content, albeit in truncated form, than your capacity to write liquid prose! Obviously this may not be true in all subjects (like English), but it is true of enough to mean that you should be able to do it.

Try to see it from an examiner's point of view. Here are two examples. The second took *three* times longer to write than the first, yet which gives more information?

Increasing opportunites for info. *access
Info. managers change viewpoint:
eg — 5 years ago OSI (open Systems Interconnection) considered more trouble than worth
NOW new technology
new software
= OSI seen as acceptable solution
5 years ago
Centralization favoured.
NOW distributed systems favoured — therefore
OSI is viable

It is interesting to observe how these increasing opportunities of access to information have caused information managers to take a different view of some problems. For instance, we now favour distributed solutions where once, as recently as five years ago, centralization was the ultimate panacea!
OSI (Open Systems Integration) is a case in point. Originally OSI seemed to pose more problems than answers, but with new technology and new software OSI is now considered to be a viable solution for information managers. More and more are adopting OSI as an information mana-

In fact, they both have the same amount of information, so if you are running out of time, your *mapping/key wording/questioning* framework will have given you the best possible training to write these note-form answers under pressure. If you are not sure whether this is acceptable, check before the exam.

11. Do your best question first to give you confidence, but don't get carried away and write and write beyond your deadline. The more you know, the more you may be inclined to do this!

12. 10-minute revision: Always do it! Many people plan to leave enough time to look over what they have done at the end, but seldom succeed. The time you spent speed reading through your whole paper will pay off. You will be surprised at how many glaring omissions, spelling errors and gaps jump out at you. Read fast but objectively. Try to feel that you are in the examiner's shoes. When you can achieve a degree of calm objectivity, you will see the gaps. Plug them, but don't try to cram in masses of superfluous material just because you remember it now.

SUMMARY

Revision is the scaffolding that supports successful exam performance. Revision should be ongoing throughout the year — daily, weekly, monthly — so that before-the-exam revision becomes a relatively effortless task of hauling material from your long-term memory to your mental current account so that you can draw it out!

No one likes exams, but better planning for exam revision can help although it will never compensate for no work during the year.

Likewise, a certain amount of panic and distress is perfectly normal at the start of an exam. By focusing on the task in hand, planning the time, planning each question, thinking it through from the examiner's point of view and ensuring that you actually do answer the question, you will help remove the exam bogey, however much you know or don't know.

Evaluating Skills

- HOW CAN I IMPROVE IF I CAN'T TELL HOW AND WHERE I NEED TO IMPROVE?
- I HAVE REALLY BAD PROBLEMS WITH STUDY : WHAT CAN I DO?

OVERVIEW

This section makes two main points:

1. It helps you to regard your learning and what results from it as a performance.
2. You are your own best judge but also your own most critical critic. To get a realistic appraisal of your performance as a learner you need to work in partnership with others — teachers, lecturers, peers, partners, friends — and this appraisal needs to be ongoing.

You judge yourself *as you go along.*

Do not wait for poor exam results at the end to tell you something.

You use other people to help you appraise your own performance. There is nothing more infuriating to teachers at any level than dumb bunnies — students who stare blankly when asked if they understand; students who clearly need help but won't take it even when it is proffered; students whose sole aim appears to be invisibility; students whose concept of being a student is akin to passive, blank blotting paper! There are some teachers who like to lecture and do not listen, but the vast majority will not only listen, but will take your anxieties seriously (provided that it is not left until the last week/night before the exam!).

Formative (ongoing) and summative (final) evaluation are both integral to self-appraisal, but you need hooks, prompts, a framework to guide you, just as you have throughout the study process. It takes discipline and regular, planned, systematic work to build self-appraisal into your study routine.

HOW CAN I IMPROVE IF I CAN'T TELL HOW AND WHERE I NEED TO IMPROVE?

1. PRODUCTS

When you start a course, check what you will be expected to *produce:*

- essays
- tests
- term papers
- tutorial presentations
- exams.

2. CRITERIA

When you know what will be required of you, ask 'What makes a good (essay, etc)?' and write a list:

GOOD [essay]	POOR [essay]
• Good intro. • Clear structure • Strong main points/arguments • Clear/sufficient supporting data • accurate • Easy to read • Short sentences • No verbosity/jargon • Good style • Good presentation	• Vague & difficult to get into • Muddled and shapeless • Waffly & vague • Too little info. • Points not substantiated with evidence • Long, windy, boring • Messy, hard to read, poor grammar/spelling

The criteria do not change much for any of the above.

3. DIAGNOSIS

If you are unsure, ask for help. 'Look, I'm still a bit confused with all this. I've written down what I think is important. Could you tell me if I'm on the right track? It could save a lot of time before I start the paper, and make it less horrible for you to mark!'

4. EXAMPLES

Collect *examples, models* — your work and others'. Try to have one model of each presentation method listed in 1, i.e. a good essay, an example of a good exam answer. If you truly don't know, ask your teacher/lecturer/tutor to show you what he/she means by good/acceptable/totally unacceptable.

5. EVALUATE

There are usually two points of evaluation : content and presentation. Basically the content must be *enough* and *accurate*, and the presentation needs to be appropriate to the purpose of what you are producing. For example, a highly emotive diatribe would not be appropriate if you have been asked to 'analyse the factors contributing to ...' If you develop your own continuum you will force yourself to rethink 'What makes a good presentation?' and this is a good thing! Using a ready-made grid (see template) which is an all-purpose guide takes less time but does not teach you as much.

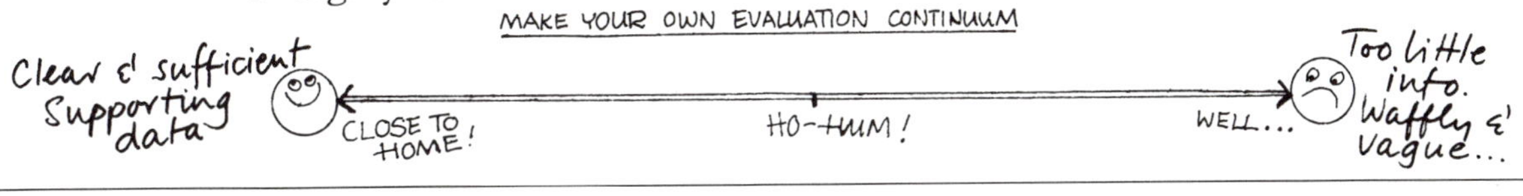

6. USE THIS BOOK

Using any of the sections in this book will provide you with a focus for evaluating your own learning performance. If you feel you are under-achieving, ask yourself the following questions:

- Your self-perception as a learner? A stunted view of learning and its demands? Your self-esteem? Inability to see what type of learner you are; to appraise your strengths and use them? Inflexibility — sticking to the sort of learning you think is the 'right' sort?

- Your self-management? Failure to plan, keep records, evaluate regularly, revise daily, weekly, monthly? Failure to recognise that your body has needs, such as food, rest, relaxation, sleep, recreation?

- Your time management? Do you know it in theory but fail in practice? Do you procrastinate, avoid all work till just before the deadline, work in horrendous all-nighters and then do nothing till the next deadline looms? Are you normal?

- Can you plan so that you know what you want to do, where you are going, when and how? Are you trying to do too much? Do you set realistic goals and objectives?

- Do you consciously make your mind muscles stretch to meet the demands you are making? Do you try to see how it all fits together by mapping it in some way? Do you list pros and cons, compare your data, work on ways to make it stick in your mind, etc?

- Have you got to the stage where you practise these skills so regularly that they become a routine, a habit? Or do they still feel strange and uncomfortable?

- Have you consciously tried to improve your reading speed and retention by using a formula like the *5S formula* (scan, skim, select, slurp, summarise)? Or do you just plod along hoping that one reading will leave an indelible deposit on your memory?

- Do you ask yourself at each stage of the six-stage research process how well you did at this stage? Do you use the checklist?

- Do you still have wads of indecipherable notes, photocopies, and handouts, or are you systematic about summarising, indexing and filing your notes daily, weekly, monthly?

- Are you good at all of this but hopeless when it comes to writing or presenting it? Is this because you don't know it, or that you lack the frameworks to act as scaffolding, and it all seems to have sunk into a heap of sludge in the bottom of your brain? Are you trying to build a skyscraper without scaffolding? Familiarity breeds contempt! It is easy to *understand* the theory of scaffolding (doing maps, key wording, formulating questions, etc), but not to practise it once it is familiar. Do you *assume* scaffolding?

- Do you bomb out under pressure? Have you been meticulous about brief but regular revision, notes, summaries, structures, planning? Can you plan your time so that you have plenty of sleep and relaxation as well as work? Can you *plan* your exam performance, predict and practise answering questions, and simulate exam conditions so that you get used to them?

- Finally, the question to ask yourself, on a regular basis is *not* 'How bad am I? How far have I got to go to be good?' but '*How much, and specifically what, have I improved since my last essay/exam/whatever?*' You are *never* going to be 100% good all of the time, but what you can, should and must aim for is to improve all of the time; to build on your strengths, use them quite consciously, and, equally consciously, acknowledge and set out to overcome your limitations.

And by the time you can answer 'Yes' to all of this, you will be a candidate for sainthood, and a very boring person! Don't aim for perfection! Just aim to be a little better, do a little better.

I HAVE REALLY BAD PROBLEMS WITH STUDY : WHAT CAN I DO?

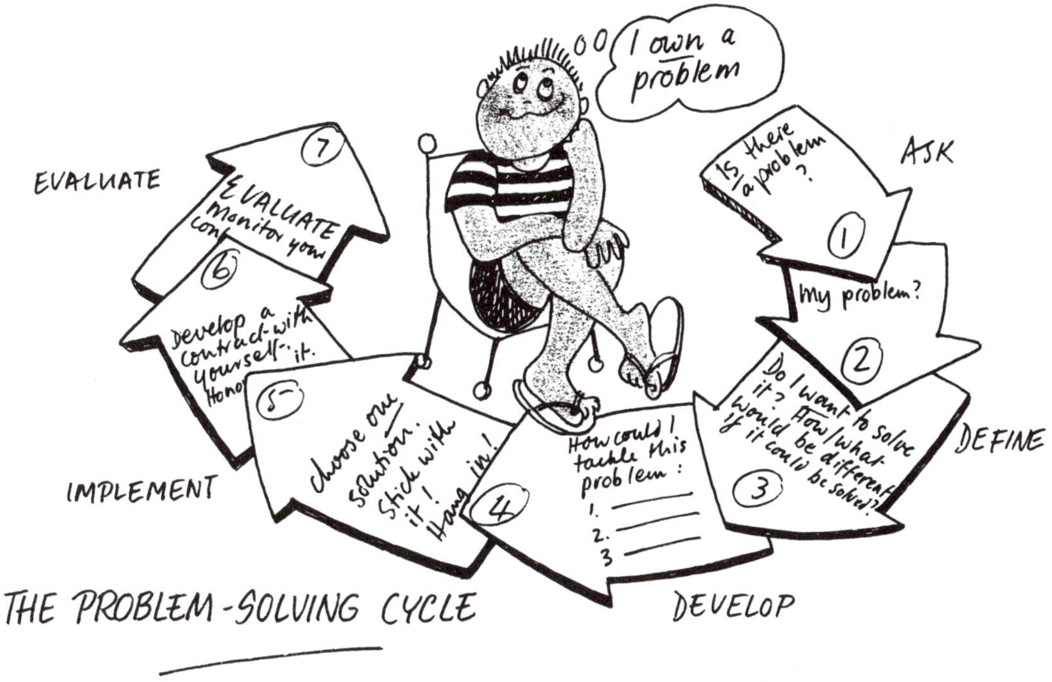

1. If you think you have a problem with learning, is it *one* problem or a whole bundle of them? The first step is to *write* it down. 'The problem is that ... '	
2. The next step is to ask what has caused it. Is is *your* problem or does the problem actually belong to someone else? If it *is* your problem, run down the causes you have listed and ask yourself whether they are within your control or not. Maybe you have listed 'lack of time'. This might well be lack of time management skills on your part, but it may well be that you simply cannot *make* enough time to do what you want to do — you have a job and a partner and a family, car, garden and shabby house. In this case there is no point in blaming yourself or thinking that your poor performance in the last lot of exams was because you are stupid.	
3. Do you actually *want* to change or solve your problem(s)? What would be/feel/look different if you did? Can you actually describe it?	

4. How could you solve it? Write down *several* ways you could tackle this problem, and then work out exactly what each solution would entail in terms of giving up, paying, stopping, starting, changing? What is actually stopping you?

5. You cannot adopt every solution. You need to choose *one* that you feel is realistic and *stick with it.* Many people have a spurt of good intentions and try to implement a whole lot of solutions at once, ending up by giving up all of them. Don't fall into this trap – start small, but hang in!

6. *Plan* to implement the solution. Write yourself a contract and work out rewards and punishments for when you succeed and fail. Monitor yourself daily.

7. Set yourself a limited timeframe. Try it for a week ... evaluate, try it for another week ... evaluate. If you are not convinced that you are solving the problem (remembering that solving most problems is a long-term process, not an instant quick-fix) you might plan to try another one of the solutions you first thought about.

Problem-solving, self-evaluation and performance appraisal are closely related. You might find that the self-appraisal checklist on P.129 is enough to show you where you are weak. But problem-solving is more precise. You need to describe a problem quite specifically. You do not say, 'I'm not a good student because I'm dumb'. That *is* dumb! You might say, 'I'm not doing as well as I might because I can't concentrate. My problem seems to be that I spend time studying but my mind wanders and I daydream, and I honestly could not tell you afterwards what I did for that hour or two.'

The point about seeing a situation as a problem is that it enables you to pinpoint exactly what is wrong and devise the solution yourself. The challenge really lies in *finding and defining the problem precisely enough* for the solution to become obvious to you. People often ask for help without first working out what the problem is and taking ownership of it.

If you do not own the problem, it is easy to rationalise it, to say 'Yes, but ...', 'I've never been good at that ...', 'But so and so doesn't do that and she ...', 'I wasn't taught that at school ...', 'I'm no good at that sort of thing ...', 'The teacher/lecturer/tutor is lousy/boring/unfocused/speaks too fast/expects too much ...'. If you do not own the problem it is all too easy to see the solutions you are being given as the fault of the person trying to help you!

Try this. Complete this in writing. One problem

I have with learning is ....

....

and then complete the checklist on the next page.

MY PROBLEM IS THAT ...	YOU COULD TRY ...
I procrastinate and then I have to do it in a rush.	Pages 15, 31, 33, 79
I try to organise myself but my notes are a jumble.	Pages 93, 95
I get carried away and write masses.	Pages 102 - 107
I find it difficult to explain clearly and concisely.	Pages 104
I find it difficult to see the point and stick to it.	Pages 108
I can't remember what we're doing from week to week.	Pages 36 - 38
We get all these reading lists, but I can't cope.	Pages 71, 72
All the books are on desk loan. I don't have the time to read them properly.	Pages 78, 79, 80
I can't find anything in libraries.	Pages 80, 83
The lectures are so boring that I just go to sleep.	Pages 90, 92, 93
I think I know it, but I can't explain it well.	Pages 112 - 114
Unless I do it all at the last minute, I forget it.	Pages 119, 120, 64 - 67
My life is too hectic to plan regular work schedules.	Pages 15, 16, 21
I only really find it easy to learn by looking — by seeing someone do something — not using my head.	Pages 4, 7, 9, 11, 17
I just don't have enough time.	Pages 32, 33, 14, 21
I find it difficult to work out what they want.	Pages 54, 36, 37, 128, 129
I hate libraries and librarians.	Pages 83
I can never find enough information.	Pages 82, 83
I've never been able to write well.	Pages 86, 87, 105, 128
I can't remember dates and things like that.	Pages 51, 60
I can't spell.	Pages 105
I know I'm untidy. I guess I always have been.	Pages 105, 106
I think I'm doing OK, but I get lousy marks.	Pages 120, 123
I hate exams. They're unfair. They're just out to trick you.	Pages 118, 128, 129
All the stuff I hand in looks a mess.	Pages 109, 110

Now try to diagnose your own problems and use the book to find a possible solution:

MY PROBLEM IS THAT ...	I COULD TRY ...

If you have got this far, you have the most precious learning commodity of all,

PERSISTENCE

so, GOOD LUCK!

SUMMARY

This section provides a summary for the whole book because it demonstrates how each of the 11 previous sections provides the signposts for asking self-evaluation questions. By evaluating your own performance as a learner *as you go along* you can pinpoint where you need to improve. If you really think you have bad problems with learning, you can implement a more precise seven-stage problem-solving cycle, defining and owning your problem, developing and testing solutions, evaluating your progress. Above all else, learning to learn involves persistence, commitment and self-knowledge.

SELF-EVALUATION GRID : TEMPLATE

CONTENT

Total accuracy.

Outstanding quantity and quality of information.

Evidence, if sought, of ability to interpret information, draw substantiated conclusions.

Evidence to support main points.

Question answered with adequate information.

Too little information/ shallow.

Off the point, but some evidence of knowledge.

Some inaccuracies.

Vague, insubstantial waffle.

Major inaccuracies. No evidence of familiarity with topic.

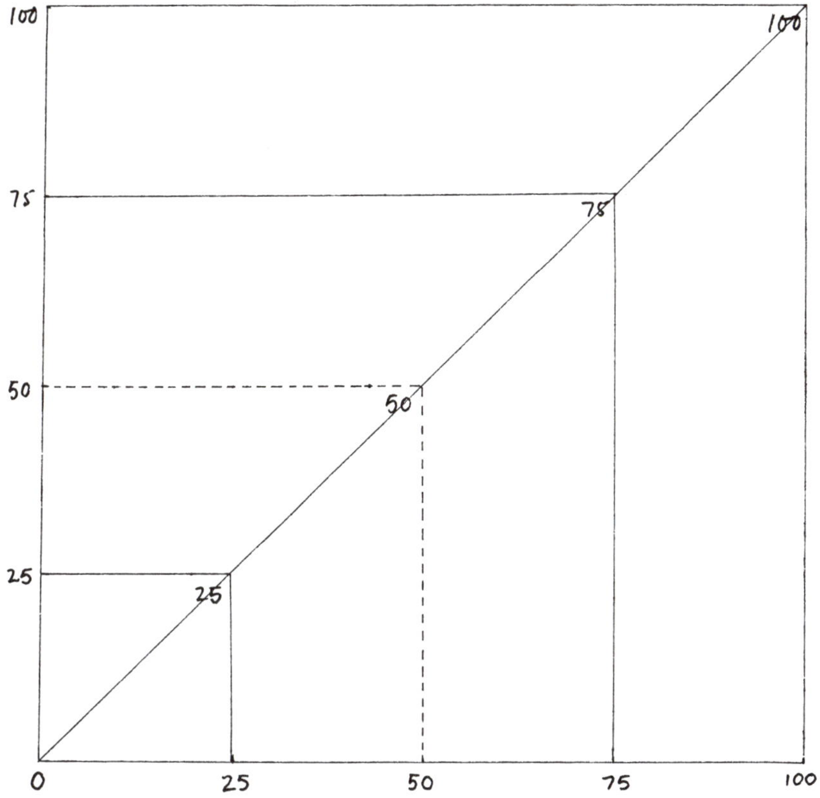

A total mess! No structure, vague, impenetrable. Poor writing, poor spelling, messy layout. Impossible to read.

A bit woolly and lacking in structure. Jargon abounds Meaning unclear. Long, verbose sentences.

Good structure. Good main points and development of sustaining argument/data. Well-written. Short crisp sentences. No jargon or waffle. Enjoyable to read.

Brilliant! Clear, logical structure. Interesting and varied style. Original, lively, challenging. A wonderful read!

PRESENTATION/STYLE

How to use it: The longitudinal axis is a very rough indication of where *content* (your actual knowledge) strengths and weaknesses might rank you. The horizontal axis looks at where your strengths and weaknesses in clarity and style of *presentation* might rank you. You can use this grid in two ways:

1. When you have done a draft of an essay or paper, read it and try to rank it on this grid. Then compare your ranking with the mark you got. If there is a discrepancy, ask your lecturer/ teacher/tutor for feedback.

2. Try to justify an exam mark using the grid. It may help you to self-evaluate.